BIRTHDAY CAKES

Skyhorse Publishing books may be purchased in bulk at special discounts for sales promotion, corporate gifts, fund-raising, or educational purposes. Special editions can also be created to specifications. For details, contact the Special Sales Department, Skyhorse Publishing, 307 West 36th Street, 11th Floor, New York, NY 10018 or info@skyhorsepublishing.com.

Skyhorse® and Skyhorse Publishing® are registered trademarks of Skyhorse Publishing, Inc.®, a Delaware corporation.

www.skyhorsepublishing.com

10 9 8 7 6 5 4 3 2 1

Library of Congress Cataloging-in-Publication Data is available on file.

Print ISBN: 978-1-62914-692-8
Ebook ISBN: 978-1-62914-873-1

Printed in China

JANNE JENSEN

BIRTHDAY CAKES

50 Traditional and Themed Cakes for Fun and Festive Birthdays

Photos: Veslemøy Vråskar

Skyhorse Publishing

CONTENTS

FOREWORD

My greatest hobby and passion is baking and decorating cakes. One of the reasons I love this is because the possibilities are nearly endless—the only limit is really just your imagination. I can be creative, and that's what makes it such fun.

That said, there's no use in making impressive, beautiful-looking cakes if they don't taste good. What lies beneath the decorations on the beautiful cake is just as important. In this book, you'll find recipes for all of my favorite cakes. My cakes have always been well-liked by adults and children alike. They're family-friendly and will appeal to just about anyone.

Everyone can learn to decorate cakes beautifully and in this book I'll teach you some fundamental techniques that you can use to impress guests at your next party. I hope I can inspire you to make your own fantastic cakes!

Oslo, January 2013

Janne Jensen

HELPFUL TIPS
FOR BAKING

GENERAL TIPS

It's nice to have a list of good tips that make your baking, and the final product, a success. Here are my best tips for baking cakes.

♥ All the ingredients should be room temperature before you begin to bake. Take them out of the refrigerator about an hour before you begin baking.

♥ Have all your ingredients and tools ready at hand before you start.

♥ Read the recipes carefully, and don't be sloppy with measurements. Be precise.

♥ Preheat the oven. It takes about 15 minutes before it gets hot.

♥ Remember to grease your pans well. Line your pans with parchment paper, so you can avoid ending up with a cake that won't let go of its pan when you're ready to take it out.

♥ Use oven shelves when you bake cakes in pans. Baking sheets can result in poor circulation in the oven.

♥ Don't open the oven door until at least half of the baking time has elapsed. That way, you'll avoid having your cake collapse.

♥ Cover the pan with a bit of parchment paper if the cake begins to darken before it's finished baking.

♥ Use a skewer to check if the cake is done. Push it all the way into the cake, in the middle. If it comes out clean, the cake is done. You can also see that the cake is ready when it begins to let go of the edges of the pan.

♥ Remember that baking times are only guidelines. The exact time varies from oven to oven, and based on the size of the baking pan.

♥ If you want to avoid having your cake develop a peak in the center, you can do this: wet a small towel and wrap it around the pan. Make sure the towel doesn't dry out while the cake is baking. The cake will take somewhat longer to bake, but you're guaranteed a cake with a flat top. You'll also avoid the edges being done before the rest of the cake, which causes them to harden before the whole cake is done. The cake will, in other words, bake more evenly.

♥ Check your baking powder. Even if it hasn't expired, it doesn't always work as well once the package has been open for a few months.

♥ If the cake collapses or sinks in the middle, the cause might be too much leavening, too small a pan, too short a baking time, too cold an oven, or a cold air from an opened oven door while baking.

- ♥ If the surface of the cake is cracked, the cause might be too much leavening, too much batter in the pan, batter that's too dry or too wet, or too high an oven temperature.

- ♥ If your egg whites don't stiffen up, the cause might be a whisk that's not clean, eggs that are too old, eggs that are too cold, or egg whites and yolks that were poorly separated.

- ♥ When cooking meringue, remember that too high an oven temperature can give you a burned cake, sugar seeping out of the meringue, or meringue that's soggy in the middle.

- ♥ If your sponge cake won't rise, the cause might be that you haven't beaten the egg mixture to the right stiffness. Remember to beat it for at least ten minutes—it should be properly stiff. It's also important to place the cake in the right part of the oven. Sponge cake batter that sits out too long on the counter loses a lot of its airiness.

- ♥ White chocolate can burn, so remember that it doesn't tolerate as much heat as regular chocolate.

- ♥ Bake cakes layer by layer. That'll give you a perfect, moist cake. If you're going to bake a three-layer cake, distribute the batter in three pans of the same size, then bake. Remember, though, that not all batters can stand to wait around. Sponge cake, for example, is one kind of batter that needs to go straight into the oven.

- ♥ Let cakes cool in their pans for about ten minutes after they're done, before turning them out and onto a rack.

- ♥ Before slicing a cake into layers, let it cool, pack it in plastic, and put it in the freezer for about thirty minutes. This prevents the cake from crumbling as you cut it.

- ♥ When covering a cake with a crème, start with a thin layer around the whole cake, then put it in the refrigerator for about thirty minutes, until the crème firms up (not necessary with whipped cream cakes and sponge cakes). Then cover the cake with a second layer. That stops crumbs from getting into the crème. The first layer holds them in place.

- ♥ To achieve a nice, smooth surface on a cake, hold the spatula under warm running water, dry it off, and then draw it across the cake. Remove any excess crème that came off on the spatula. Repeat the process until you've gone over the whole cake.

- ♥ Don't put too much crème in a piping bag when applying it to a cake. It could melt from the warmth of your hands. It's best to fill the piping bag several times.

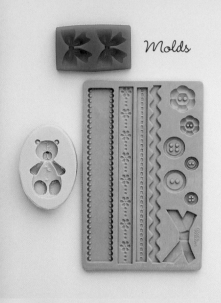

Molds

Cutters

Measuring Spoons

Kitchen Scales

Sugar Gun

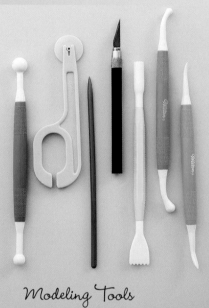

Modeling Tools

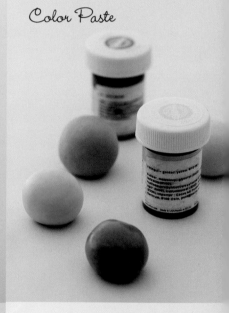

Color Paste

Spray Predictor

Dough Scraper

Spatulas

Cake Pans

Wooden Spoons

Grater

Spatula

EQUIPMENT

I recommend the following equipment for easy and successful work in the kitchen.

- Stand mixer
- Hand mixer
- Springform pan
- Two round pans, 8 inches (20 cm) in diameter
- Molds and cake pans in different styles (Wonder Mold, sports balls, squares, and daisy pans are used in this book)
- Kitchen scale
- Deciliter measuring cup
- Measuring spoons, for precise measurements
- Cooling rack
- Mixing bowls
- Colander
- Ruler/measuring tape
- Scissors
- Cake-decorating accessories
- Spatula
- Dough scraper
- Small, sharp knife, without serrations
- Cutting wheel (I use a small one for decorations, and a pizza wheel to cut around the edges when making cake coverings)
- Plastic rolling pin with rubber-size rings, for a smooth surface
- Piping bags and tips, and a few connectors, which makes it easier to change tips
- Rotating tray
- Cake smoother
- Various shape cutters
- Some modeling tools
- A sugar gun (a device that presses out fondants in various sizes and shapes)
- Paintbrushes, to paint and attach decorations on cakes
- Parchment paper
- Color pastes and powders
- Cardboard cake stand, for tiered cakes
- Wooden/plastic sticks, for tiered cakes
- Sugar thermometer (you can buy one in a hobby shop or cake store)
- Ladles, whisks, spatulas, etc.

3.

6.

8.

DIFFERENT TECHNIQUES

How to make cake tops

When rolling out cake coverings, I recommend using a plastic mat and a plastic rolling pin. You'll find that the rolling goes much more smoothly this way. You can also find rolling pins with rubber rings in three different thicknesses you can place on the ends. This guarantees a nice, smooth surface. You can find plastic mats in stores that sell kitchen equipment. Large plastic rolling pins are sold in stores that carry cake supplies. You can also visit a hardware store and buy a piece of plastic pipe in whatever length you'd like as a cheaper alternative. These pipes carry the water we drink, so there's no danger to using them.

I recommend using a cake spatula to get a fine, smooth surface for your cake covering. A spatula is a tool with a smooth surface and a handle, which you can use to stroke it across the surface to make it even and smooth.

Cover the cake with a thin layer of crème before putting on the cover. Allow about half an inch (one centimeter) of crème-free space at the bottom of the cake. That way, you'll avoid having crème pressed out and visible around the sides when the covering has been placed on the cake.

Roll out the dough so that it's 0.1–0.2 inches (0.3–0.5 millimeters) thick. There is nothing good about a covering that's way too thick. Use rubber rings to get the right thickness and a smooth surface. It's a good idea to roll the covering out to be a bit bigger than you actually need. That makes it easier to achieve a fine edge at the bottom, without lumps or creases.

Carefully lift the covering over the cake. Use a cake spatula to smooth out the top first. That will also press out any air bubbles that might be underneath. Use the palm of your right hand to bring the covering in around the cake, while using your left hand to adjust it so that the bottom edge remains straight, avoiding lumps or overlap. When you've done this all around the cake, go over it once more with the cake spatula for a flat, smooth cake.

Then, use a cutting wheel to cut off all the excess covering around the bottom of the cake.

If you're a bit unlucky when you're starting out, you can easily add a decorative border around the bottom of the cake. That'll hide any blemishes and add a decorative touch to the cake.

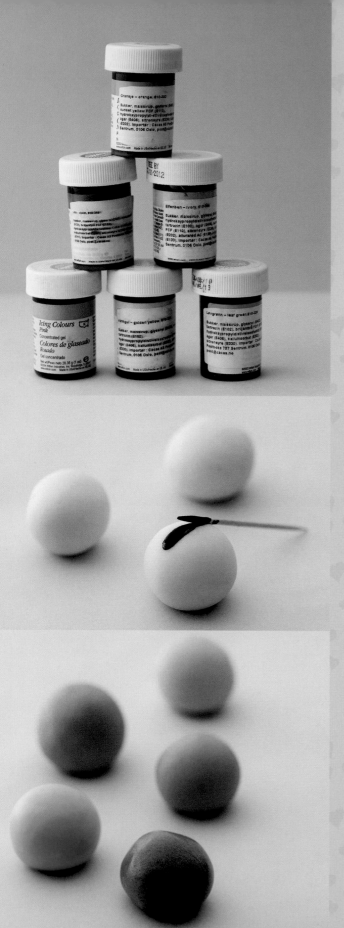

How to color fondant and marzipan

When coloring fondant and marzipan, you've got to experiment a bit to find the color you want. I find that marzipan often takes on color quicker than homemade fondant, since it's lighter. When you color fondant or marzipan, it's best to use color paste. It's thicker in consistency than ordinary food coloring. If you use food coloring, you'll end up with a sticky, useless mass. The color pastes are highly concentrated, so a little bit goes a long way.

Start by getting a bit of the color on the tip of a knife or drink stirrer, and smooth it over the substance you want to color. Then begin kneading the color into the substance. If you find that the color is getting too light, simply add more. But remember that it doesn't take a whole lot when you're using color pastes. As I mentioned earlier, it's very concentrated, so don't use too much at once. It's easier to add than to remove.

You can also blend new colors by kneading several colors into a substance. Remember the color wheel from grade school? We learned what happens when we blend the different primary colors. Yellow and pink can, for example, produce a sort of flesh tone. Black and white make grey. Red and a touch of black can give you a deeper shade of red, and so on. Remember to write down what and how much you use if you blend your way to a great color. Then you'll remember it the next time you want to use that color. Feel free to experiment and play with the colors. You might discover a new, fantastic color by accident.

Color pastes can be easily washed off with water and soap, but some of the stronger colors like blue and black can be more difficult to remove. For that reason, it's a good idea to keep disposable gloves on hand in your kitchen. You can buy these at the pharmacy, or in an ordinary grocery store.

Note that black and red are difficult colors to blend when it comes to fondant or other white substances—it takes a lot of color. If you want to use these, I'd recommend coloring the substance a day in advance, since the colors typically set better once they've sat for a bit. At any rate, I'm never quite satisfied with the result. It's easier to color plain marzipan with red and black.

How to paint on fondant and use powdered colors.

There are lots of exciting powder colors including plain, metallic, and glossy colors.

You can paint with color powders. Put a few drops of rejuvenator spirit (a special kind of spirit) in a small bowl. You can buy it in cake shops. You can also replace it with a bit of vodka. Take a bit of the powder color on the brush and stir it into the rejuvenator or alcohol until the color becomes even. Then you can paint on the cake or decorations. The reason behind using vodka is that alcohol evaporates quickly, so the color will also dry quickly.

Powder colors are also great on decorations without mixing them with rejuvenator spirit. This is especially true of glossy powder. Use a round brush and spread the powder evenly over the surface you want to cover. It's a bit like using makeup, and is often called "dusting."

You can also paint with color pastes stirred into a bit of water, but remember not to make it too wet, or it could destroy your covering.

For small details and writing, you can use color pens. You can buy markers with edible ink in lots of different colors. I've used these for the cut-out of Winnie the Pooh (see the cake on page 92), since lots of the details are small and easier to draw with a marker.

A good tip is to cover a cake with a white covering, then give brushes and colors to the birthday boy or girl—it's fun to decorate your own birthday cake!

How to make tiered cakes

Making a tiered cake is easy and doesn't require too much extra equipment. What's important to remember is that a stable cake is made with sticks and cardboard cake dishes so that the cake doesn't collapse.

Make two cakes, e.g. one that's 8 inches (20 cm) in diameter, and one that's 6 inches (15 cm). Fill the cakes and cover them with a cake covering if you want one. If not, cover them with a crème.

The cake on top needs a cake board underneath it. Cake boards made of cardboard can be bought in shops that sell cake equipment, or you can check with a local baker. A thin piece of cardboard is all it takes. The cake board needs to be the same diameter as the cake itself, so that the board isn't visible.

The bottommost cake needs a few sticks. Since it's only two tiers, three sticks in a triangle in the center of the cake are enough. The second cake rests on top of the sticks.

There are also several kinds of sticks. Shops that sell cake equipment sell something known as plastic dowel rods, which you can use as supports in your cake. Hobby shops sell long, untreated wooden sticks about the same thickness as a straw. Both plastic and wooden sticks are long, but you can cut them to whatever length you like. You can also stick straws with skewers inside into the bottom of the cake, forming a triangle in the middle, so that the sticks hold the top tier up. What's important is that you use something untreated that can be in contact with food without causing any damage.

You can determine how long the stick needs to be by placing it next to the cake and measuring it. It should be as tall as the cake. Mark the stick with a pen or pencil. Cut three sticks of equal lengths and push them down into the cake in a triangle at the center, so that the sticks hold the top tier up. Cover the holes with a crème or whatever other substance you've used to cover the rest of your cake.

Place the smaller cake in the center of the bigger cake. If you have a hard time eyeballing the center of the cake, measure it and make some small marks where the cake will be placed.

Cover the edge around the top cake with a decorative pattern to cover the division between the two cakes. Now the cake is ready to be decorated and served.

TIP

You can choose whether you'd like to decorate each cake individually and then put them together, or assemble them first, and then decorate. If you're going to take the cake somewhere, it's more practical to decorate the cake first and assemble it where the cake will be served.

How to make cake cutouts

A puzzle plaque is a great decoration for a cake, and you don't need very much equipment to make it. The reason this is referred to as a puzzle technique is quite simply because you cut out and shape individual pieces, then put them together to make a picture, just like a jigsaw puzzle. This is a simple, useful technique for decorating cakes. You can use whatever picture you like, so choose one that's fitting for the guest of honor.

Here's what you need:

- ♥ A picture, which you'll cut into pieces. Print out an extra copy to keep whole, so that you can use it as a guide if you're not sure about small details.
- ♥ Fondant or marzipan, in the colors you'll use for the picture.
- ♥ A small cutting wheel.
- ♥ A hobby knife for small details (often called a craft knife).
- ♥ A knife.
- ♥ A bit of water or edible paste and a brush, to glue together the pieces.
- ♥ Drink stirrers or untreated toothpicks (I use these a lot; they're great for nudging small things into place).

1.

Edible Glue

Sugar Gun

2.

How to make a Winnie-the-Pooh picture

Simple figures like Winnie-the-Pooh are perfect to start with. As you improve, you can experiment with more detailed pictures.

Print out a picture from the Internet at a suitable size, or draw your own. Cut it out.

Roll out some orange fondant. Place the picture of Winnie-the-Pooh on top and cut around it with a hobby knife or small cutting wheel. That gives you the entire foundation of the bear.

Cut the picture into pieces. For this picture, I need Winnie's leg that's closest to us and his red sweater.

Place the leg on the orange fondant you've already rolled out, and use a hobby knife to cut it out. Roll out some red substance and do the same with the sweater.

Put together all the pieces, so that you get a picture; stick them together with edible glue or water. Use a pen with edible ink to draw on the details, such as the eyes, nose, eyebrows, tongue, etc.

Finally, use a sugar gun to make the black border around the figure. Use a bit of edible glue or water to attach this border to the figure.

4.

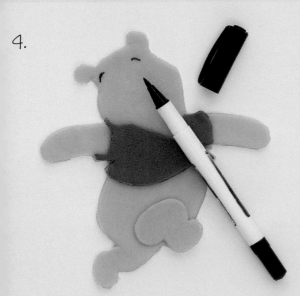

5.

21

BASIC RECIPES

BASIC RECIPES FOR CAKES

In this chapter, you'll find basic recipes for cakes and crèmes that you can combine however you like, all according to taste.

It's important to experiment with different tastes and combinations of cakes—that's how you'll discover your own favorites. You can have different layers in the same cake, too—for example, one layer banana cake, one layer chocolate cake, and one layer raspberry cake with your favorite chocolate crème between the layers. Leftover cake bases can go in the freezer, and you can take them out the next time you need them.

Cake pans

Generally, all these recipes are designed to be made in pans with a diameter of 9-10 inches (24-26 cm). I often bake my cakes in two 8-inch (20 cm) pans, since I like my cakes to be a bit tall. That's an easy way to give the cakes a bit more of a festive touch. I often get feedback about how nice and tall my cakes are and questions about how I do it. The answer is several layers baked in slightly smaller pans. I distribute the batter evenly in two pans, sometimes even three, instead of putting all of it in one bigger pan. That way, you never end up with cakes that are overdone on the sides and raw in the middle, and your cakes don't grow peaks in the middle.

You can choose if you want to have one layer of filling in the cake, or if you want to cut each cake in half horizontally, which gives you four cake bases. This also contributes to the height of a cake. To simplify the slicing, I use a cake cutter. The result is nice, even cake bases. But you can just as well use a large knife, if you can make straight slices.

Baking time

Baking times vary from oven to oven and depending on what sort of pan you're baking in. All cakes baked in pans have a baking time of 1-1½ hours. Remember that sponge cakes need less time.

If you distribute the batter among several pans, the baking time becomes 20-40 minutes. The results are best if you have a good feel for your oven and monitor the baking time the first time you bake a cake. When the cake begins to come off the edges and a toothpick or skewer comes out clean, you know the cake is done. Remember to always stick the toothpick in the middle of the cake, since that's the last part of the cake to finish cooking.

Sponge cake

Making sponge cake is easier than you might think. It's not too much work and doesn't require many ingredients. The cake can, however, be quickly destroyed if you don't follow the recipe carefully, and then you'll end up with a flat cake. The secret to a successful sponge cake is a long beating time. I beat the egg mixture for at least 10-15 minutes, so it's not a bad idea to invest in a good stand mixer. There are lots of good stand mixers that won't cost you an arm and a leg.

This recipe is designed for a pan that's 8-10 inches (20-24 cm) in diameter, but it's easy to scale the recipe up or down. For every egg you use in the batter, use one ounce (30 g) of sugar, and one ounce (30 g) of flour.

Here's what you do:

♥ Heat the oven to 350°F (175°C).
♥ Grease a cake pan that's 8-10 inches (20-24 cm) in diameter, and line the bottom with parchment paper.
♥ Beat the eggs and sugar. The mixture should be white and porous. You should be able to turn the bowl upside-down without the mixture pouring out.
♥ Sift the flour and baking powder into the mixture using a sieve to avoid lumps.
♥ Here, you've got to be very careful to avoid folding the flour into the egg mixture too quickly. That'll take all the air out of the mixture, and you'll have a flat cake. Use a spatula to fold it in carefully.
♥ Pour the batter into the greased pan. Place it directly into the oven; sponge cake doesn't take well to sitting out before baking—the cake will collapse easily.
♥ Bake the cake on the lowest rack in the oven for about 30 minutes. Don't let any cold air in while the cake is baking. The cake should become golden and is ready when it lets go of the pan. You might also use a toothpick to check if the cake is done, if you aren't sure.
♥ Let the cake cool for a bit before taking it out of the pan.

You need:

5 eggs
⅓ lb (150 g) sugar
⅓ lb (150 g) wheat flour
½ tsp baking powder

TIP
This cake takes well to being frozen.

Sponge cake with cocoa

Sponge cake with cocoa is something for all of us chocolate lovers. The cake has the same consistency as regular sponge cake, but with the taste of chocolate.

For this cake, I recommend fillings like raspberry or orange mousse or vanilla crème. Orange and raspberry taste good with chocolate, and vanilla crème goes well with just about anything.

Here's what you do:

♥ The process is the same as that for regular sponge cake. Sift the cocoa and vanilla sugar together with the flour and baking powder.

You need:

4 eggs
¼ lb (125 g) sugar
4 tbsp cocoa powder
1 tsp vanilla sugar
2 oz (50 g) wheat flour
½ tsp baking powder

Chocolate cake

This is a moist, delicious chocolate cake with a mild flavor, so it's great for young and old alike.

You need:

¼ lb (125 g) margarine/butter, at room temperature

14 oz (400 g) sugar

3 eggs

⅔ lb (300 g) wheat flour

3 tsp baking powder

3 tsp vanilla sugar

4 tbsp cocoa powder

1¼ cups (300 mL) milk

Here's what you do:

- ♥ Heat the oven to 350°F (175°C).
- ♥ Grease two baking pans, 8 inches (20 cm) in diameter. Line the bottom with parchment paper.
- ♥ Beat the margarine/butter and sugar together until it's light and airy.
- ♥ Beat in one egg at a time.
- ♥ Mix all the dry ingredients in a bowl.
- ♥ Alternate adding the dry ingredients and the milk to mix the batter.
- ♥ Distribute the batter evenly in both pans.
- ♥ Bake the cake for 30-40 minutes. Be very careful not to bake the cakes too long.
- ♥ Let the cakes cool a bit before taking them out of their pans and letting them cool completely on a rack.

TIP

If you want to make a marbled cake, you can mix chocolate cake batter and vanilla cake batter. Start by pouring some of the chocolate cake batter, then some vanilla cake batter. Repeat this once, then carefully draw a fork through the batter. Then you'll have a marbled cake.

Vanilla cake

This is a very moist, tasty vanilla cake. It should be eaten the same day it's made.

You need:

¾ lb (350 g) sugar

6 oz (175 g) margarine/butter, at room temperature

4 eggs

7 fl oz (200 mL) milk

¾ lb (325 g) wheat flour

4 tsp vanilla sugar

3 tsp baking powder

Here's what you do:

- ♥ Heat the oven to 350°F (175°C).
- ♥ Grease two cake pans, 8 inches (20 cm) in diameter, and line the bottom of each with parchment paper.
- ♥ Beat the margarine/butter and sugar together until it's light and airy.
- ♥ Beat in one egg at a time.
- ♥ Mix all the dry ingredients in a bowl.
- ♥ Alternately mix the dry ingredients and add the milk to the batter.
- ♥ Distribute the batter evenly in the two pans.
- ♥ Bake the cakes for 25-35 minutes. Be very careful to avoid baking them for too long.
- ♥ Let the cakes cool a bit before taking them out of their pans and letting them cool completely on a rack.

TIP

You can substitute a vanilla bean in place of vanilla sugar. Scrape out the seeds with a spoon and add them to the batter.

27

Raspberry or strawberry cake

You can make this a raspberry cake or a strawberry cake—the choice is yours.

You need:

½ lb (225 g) margarine/ butter, at room temperature

¾ lb (350 g) sugar

3.5 oz (100 g) raspberry or strawberry powdered gelatin

4 eggs

13 oz (375 g) wheat flour

3 tsp baking powder

3 tsp vanilla sugar

1 cup (250 mL) milk

⅓ lb (150 g) raspberries or strawberries

Optionally, a bit of red color paste, if you want to bring out the color more

Here's what you do:

♥ Heat the oven to 350°F (175°C).
♥ Grease two cake pans, 8 inches (20 cm) in diameter, and line the bottoms with parchment paper.
♥ Beat together the margarine/butter, sugar, and powdered gelatin until it's light and airy.
♥ Beat in one egg at a time.
♥ Mix all the dry ingredients in a bowl.
♥ Alternately mix the dry ingredients and add the milk to make the batter.
♥ Mash the raspberries or strawberries; use frozen berries if you can. Mix the mashed berries into the batter.
♥ Distribute the batter evenly between the two pans.
♥ Bake the cakes in the center of the oven for 35–45 minutes.
♥ Let the cakes cool a bit before taking them out of their pans and letting them cool completely on a rack.

Banana cake

Banana makes cakes extra moist and gives them an extra-delicious flavor. Chopped chocolate in a banana cake is really tasty if you want to add a little extra something.

You need:

3 eggs

1½ cups (350 mL) sugar

½ lb (225 g) margarine/butter

7 fl oz (200 mL) milk

2 cups (500 mL) wheat flour

3 tsp baking powder

3 tsp vanilla sugar

2 ripe bananas, mashed

3.5 oz (100 g) chopped chocolate or chocolate chips

Here's what you do:

♥ Heat the oven to 350°F (175°C).
♥ Grease two cake pans, 8 inches (20 cm) in diameter, and line the bottoms with parchment paper.
♥ Melt the margarine/butter in a saucepan.
♥ Beat the eggs and sugar together.
♥ Mix all the dry ingredients together, then add a bit of the milk. Beat until there are no more lumps in the batter.
♥ Add the rest of the milk and the melted margarine/butter, then blend well with the egg mixture.
♥ Finally, blend the mashed banana and chopped chocolate into the batter. Use a stand mixer to ensure it's thoroughly mixed.
♥ Bake the cakes in the center of the oven for 30–40 minutes.
♥ Let the cakes cool a bit before taking them out of their pans. Let them cool completely on a rack.

TIP

If you have a good cake recipe, you can also use it to make muffins. Simply pour the batter into a muffin mold instead of a big cake pan. Remember to shorten the baking time.

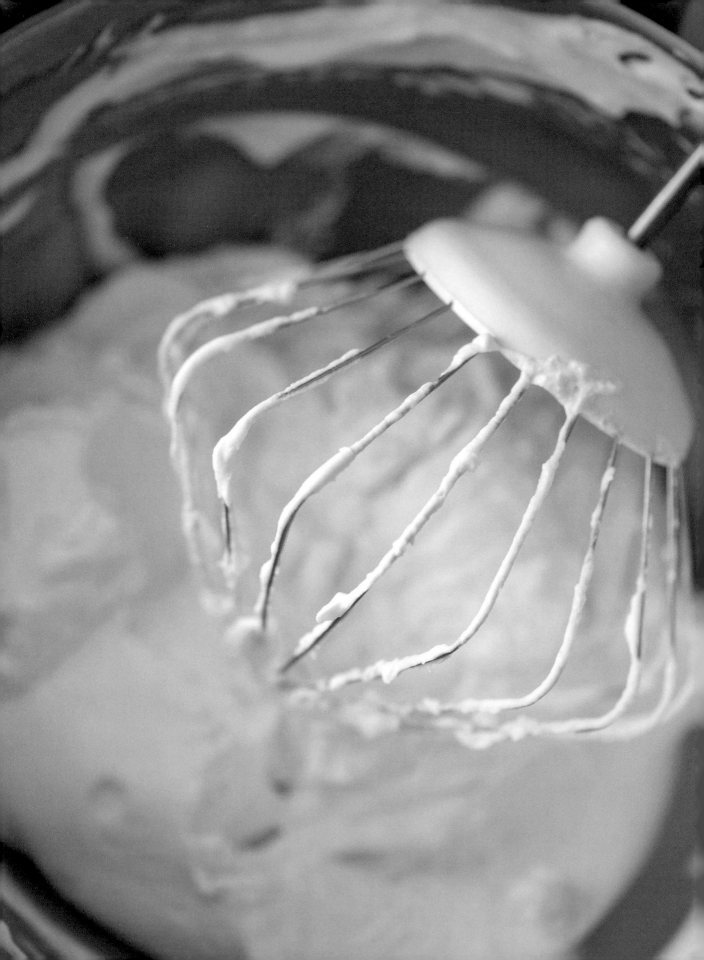

BASIC RECIPES FOR CRÈMES AND FILLINGS

In my butter creams, I prefer margarine instead of butter; in my opinion, the flavor is better and not so overpowering. If you love butter, you can use half butter and half margarine. If you only use butter, you can end up with a cream that's overpowering and a bit nauseating.

White butter cream

The advantage of using white butter cream is that you can color it with color pastes. You can also add different flavors.

You need:

9 oz (250 g) margarine/butter, at room temperature

1 lb (500 g) powdered sugar

3 tsp vanilla sugar

3–4 tbsp milk

Here's what you do:

♥ Put all the ingredients into a stand mixer.
♥ Beat for a good while until you have a nice, fluffy butter cream.

Chocolate butter cream

This cream is useful and goes well with most cakes.

You need:

9 oz (250 g) margarine/ butter, at room temperature

1 lb (500 g) powdered sugar

3 tbsp cocoa powder

1 tsp vanilla sugar

4 tbsp milk (you can also use coffee or liquor, if the cake's for adults)

Here's what you do:

♥ Put all the ingredients into a stand mixer.
♥ Beat for a good while until you have a nice, fluffy butter cream.

TIP

If you want to make a black cream, you have to use chocolate butter cream as the base, and then add black coloring. Normal butter cream is difficult to make black enough.

Chocolate Butter Cream

Strawberry Butter Cream

TIPS

Feel free to use more strawberries or raspberries for a more intense flavor.

Butter cream with raspberries or strawberries

This is a butter cream that takes on a more fresh flavor with berries. If your purée gets too runny, you'll get better results by straining off much of the juice. If the cream is too thin, add more powdered sugar.

You need:

13 oz (375 g) margarine/ butter, at room temperature

1 lb (500 g) powdered sugar

3 tsp vanilla sugar

3.5 lb (100 g) frozen strawberries or raspberries

Here's what you do:

♥ Blend the margarine, powdered sugar, and vanilla sugar into a smooth mass in a stand mixer.
♥ Make a purée out of the frozen strawberries or raspberries. Make sure the purée isn't too thin. If it's too thin, strain off some of the liquid.
♥ Mix the butter cream and berry purée. Beat for a good while, so the cream becomes fluffy.

Chocolate crème

This crème is unbelievably tasty and airy, since it's made with a mixture of sugar and eggs. You can use whatever kind of chocolate you like for this recipe: milk chocolate, chocolate with nuts, dark chocolate, all depending on your own taste.

You need:

7 oz (200 g) chocolate

2 eggs

⅓ lb (150 g) powdered sugar

7 oz (200 g) margarine/ butter, at room temperature

Here's what you do:

♥ Melt the chocolate in the microwave or in a warm water bath. Let it cool.
♥ Beat the eggs and powdered sugar together.
♥ Then beat the room-temperature margarine/butter into the egg mixture.

HERE'S HOW YOU MELT CHOCOLATE OVER A WATER BATH:

♥ Break the chocolate into pieces and place them in a heat-proof bowl.
♥ Place the bowl over a saucepan with hot, simmering water. Make sure the bottom of the bowl isn't touching the water.
♥ When the chocolate begins to melt, carefully stir it until it's even and smooth. Take the bowl off the heat and let it cool a little.

HERE'S HOW YOU MELT CHOCOLATE IN A MICROWAVE OVEN:

♥ Break the chocolate into pieces and place them in a microwave-safe bowl.
♥ Place the bowl in the microwave for one minute. Take it out and stir the chocolate. Put it back in for 30 more seconds. Stir until it's even and smooth. If the chocolate isn't completely melted just yet, put it back in for another 30 seconds.
♥ Let it cool.

White chocolate crème

You can color this crème with color pastes if you want to make vibrant, colorful cakes.

You need:

7 oz (200 g) white chocolate

2 eggs

⅓ lb (150 g) powdered sugar

7 oz (200 g) margarine/ butter, at room temperature

Here's what you do:

♥ Melt the chocolate in the microwave or over a water bath. Let it cool.
♥ Beat the eggs and powdered sugar together.
♥ Then beat in the room-temperature margarine/butter. Beat it for a good while, so the crème is lump-free, light, and airy.
♥ Finally, add the melted chocolate. Beat it until it's thoroughly mixed with the rest of the crème. The longer you beat it, the fluffier the crème will be.

TIP

White chocolate can't tolerate as much heat as regular chocolate, so when you melt it, make sure it doesn't get too hot, or it could burn. The safest way to melt it is using a water bath.

Cheese crème

Cheese crème is good for various kinds of cakes. Experiment, and perhaps you'll find a new favorite.

You need:

7 oz (200 g) plain cream cheese

7 oz (200 g) margarine/ butter, at room temperature

14 oz (400 g) powdered sugar

Here's what you do:

♥ Beat the cream cheese, margarine/butter, and powdered sugar into a smooth crème in a stand mixer.

TIPS

♥ Always use regular cream cheese. If you use light cream cheese, you'll end up with a grainy crème.
♥ Use chocolate cream cheese instead of plain cream cheese for a chocolate cheese crème.
♥ Add 3.5 oz (100 g) melted white chocolate for a white chocolate cheese crème.
♥ The cheese crème will have a somewhat fresher flavor if you add the zest of an orange or lemon and a little fresh-squeezed orange or lemon juice.

Swiss meringue butter cream

This is a delicious, fluffy butter cream that's not as sweet as normal white butter cream.

You need:

3 egg whites

½ lb (225 g) sugar

2 tsp vanilla sugar

¾ lb (325 g) margarine/butter, at room temperature

Here's what you do:

♥ Mix the egg whites and sugar in a heat-proof bowl.
♥ Place the bowl over a saucepan with boiling water, but remember to keep the bowl from touching the water.
♥ Beat continuously, so that the egg whites don't form clumps.
♥ Warm the egg whites and sugar to 140°F (60°C); use a sugar thermometer.
♥ Next, place the egg whites in the bowl of a stand mixer and beat them until they've cooled to room temperature.
♥ Add the vanilla sugar and margarine/butter in small pieces, a bit at a time, and beat until the crème is nice and airy.

TIPS

♥ You can add a chocolate flavor to this butter cream by adding 3.5 oz (100 g) melted, cooled chocolate.
♥ Add about 3.5 oz (about 100 g) mashed raspberries or strawberries. Strain off the seeds so that the crème is smoother.
♥ Add 3.5 oz (100 g) plain or chocolate-flavored cream cheese for a cream cheese flavor.
♥ Add about 3.5 oz (about 100 g) orange crème for a fresh orange flavor.
♥ Add 2 tbsp powdered coffee, dissolved in warm water, for a coffee flavor.

Orange crème

This crème is fresh and tasty. It's good with ganache. It takes some time to make this crème, since you've got to stand around and stir it for a bit, but it's absolutely worth it.

You need:

2 oranges

the juice of half a lime

¼ lb (125 g) margarine/butter, preferably unsalted

7 oz (200 g) sugar

3 eggs, beaten

Here's what you do:

- ♥ Zest one of the oranges. Remember to avoid the white part, which has a bitter flavor.
- ♥ Juice the oranges until you have 1 cup (250 mL) of juice.
- ♥ Place the orange juice and orange zest in a small saucepan, and let it boil until you're left with about $^2/_5$ cup (about 100 mL).
- ♥ Add the lime juice.
- ♥ Mix all the ingredients—margarine/butter, sugar, beaten eggs, and juice—in a metal bowl. Place the bowl over a saucepan with water in it; keep it just under the boiling point. Remember to keep the bowl from touching the water.
- ♥ Stir continuously, until the crème thickens and has reached a good consistency. This should take about 20 minutes.
- ♥ Let the crème cool. It has to be stored in the fridge.

Lemon crème

This is a fresh, delicious crème. Try it with sponge cake, alongside strawberries and cream.

You need:

3 eggs

7 oz (200 g) sugar

zest and juice of 1 lemon

2 oz (50 g) margarine/butter

2 tsp powdered gelatin + 4 tbsp water/lemon juice

Here's what you do:

- ♥ Mix the eggs, sugar, lemon zest, lemon juice, and margarine/butter in a metal bowl. Place it over a water bath.
- ♥ Beat vigorously until the crème is thick and fluffy.
- ♥ Distribute the powdered gelatin in a small saucepan. Let it sit for 5 minutes. Heat the pan and stir until all the powder is dissolved. Add the dissolved gelatin to the crème and stir it until everything's thoroughly mixed.
- ♥ Let the crème cool.

Ganache

Ganache is a crème composed of two ingredients—cream and chocolate. You can flavor it with coffee or liquor. You can use it as a filling or icing on a cake. If you use it as icing and cool it down for a while, it's great to use under a covering. It gets a bit stiffer than normal cream, which makes for a covering that's straighter and prettier.

You need:

½ cup (125 mL) cream

7 oz (200 g) cooking chocolate

Here's what you do:

♥ Pour the cream into a saucepan and heat it to its boiling point. Take the saucepan off the heat.
♥ Add the chocolate in pieces; stir until the chocolate has melted into the cream.
♥ Let the cream cool until spreadable.
♥ You can also beat the crème to obtain a fluffier variant.

White ganache

This recipe is like regular ganache, but the chocolate is replaced by white chocolate. You can also add chopped raspberries if you'd like a fresher flavor.

You need:

5 fl oz (150 mL) cream

⅔ lb (300 g) white chocolate

optionally, ¼ lb (125 g) fresh raspberries, chopped

Here's what you do:

♥ Pour the cream into a saucepan and heat it to its boiling point. Take the saucepan off the heat.
♥ Add the chocolate in pieces, and stir until the chocolate has melted into the cream.
♥ Let the crème cool until it's spreadable.
♥ You can also beat the crème to obtain a fluffier variant.

Chocolate icing

This crème is quite similar to ganache, but some margarine/butter is added to it so it has a softer, rounder flavor. This chocolate crème is strong, but delicious.

You need:

5 fl oz (150 mL) cream

7 oz (200 g) cooking chocolate, in pieces

2 oz (50 g) margarine/butter

Here's what you do:

♥ Pour the cream into a saucepan and heat it to its boiling point. Take the pan off the heat.
♥ Add the chocolate and margarine/butter, and stir until the chocolate has melted into the cream.
♥ Let the crème cool until spreadable.

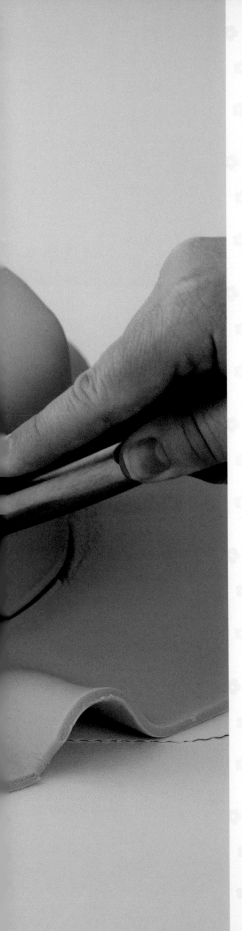

DECORATING MATERIALS

When I'm going to top a cake, there are three materials I prefer to work with, all of which taste great. One is marzipan, which I recommend buying. The second is fondant, and the third is chocolate paste, which is great if you want to have a chocolate cover for your cake.

Many wonder whether or not you can use marzipan to cover a chocolate cake, and the answer is, absolutely yes! Chocolate and marzipan are delicious together.

In addition to fondant, I've included a recipe for modeling paste in this book. Modeling paste is good to make decorations out of. The white substances take well to coloring with color pastes.

Tragacanth or CMC (Carboxymethyl cellulose) is used in modeling paste to make the paste more elastic and able to retain its shape. It's not necessary for making coverings, but important if you want to make decorations. You can buy tragacanth at the pharmacy, and CMC is sold in stores that specialize in cake equipment. CMC is a cheaper alternative to tragacanth, essentially being chemically-prepared tragacanth.

Fondant

You can add flavorings to fondant, and if you choose to go that route, use 4 tbsp water and skip the lemon juice.

You need:

1 tbsp powdered gelatin

1 tbsp water

3 tbsp lemon juice

2 tsp vanilla sugar

about 1 lb, 14 oz (about 850 g) powdered sugar

½ cup (125 mL) light treacle

1 oz (30 g) hardened coconut butter

Here's what you do:

♥ Sprinkle the gelatin powder in a small saucepan, and cover it with the water and lemon juice. Let sit for 5 minutes.
♥ Put the vanilla sugar and powdered sugar in a stand mixer with a dough hook attachment.
♥ Put the saucepan containing the gelatin on a burner and heat it up. Stir until the gelatin has dissolved. Add the treacle and coconut butter and stir until the coconut butter has dissolved.
♥ Add the liquid to the stand mixer; let the mixer knead everything until it's thoroughly mixed.
♥ The substance should be sticky; it takes some time for it to develop fully.
♥ Wrap the substance completely with plastic wrap and place it in the fridge until the next day.
♥ Now the fondant is ready to use. Take it out of the fridge a few hours before you want to use it, so that it can reach room temperature. Knead it well before rolling it out. If it's still a bit sticky, knead it in a bit of powdered sugar.
♥ Color the fondant with coloring paste.

You need:

1 tbsp powdered gelatin

4 tbsp water

2 tsp vanilla sugar

1.5 oz (40 g) cocoa powder

about 1 lb, 5 oz (600 g) powdered sugar

½ cup (125 mL) light treacle

1 oz (30 g) hardened coconut oil

Fondant with cocoa

This is a variant of fondant with a chocolate flavor.

Here's what you do:

♥ Sprinkle the gelatin powder in a small saucepan and cover it with water. Let it sit for 5 minutes.
♥ Put the vanilla sugar, cocoa powder, and powdered sugar in a stand mixer with a kneading hook.
♥ Put the saucepan containing the gelatin on a burner and heat it up. Stir until the gelatin has dissolved. Add the treacle and coconut butter, and stir until the coconut butter has melted.
♥ Add the liquid to the stand mixer, and let it be kneaded until everything is thoroughly mixed.
♥ The substance should be sticky, as it takes some time for it to fully develop.
♥ Pack the substance completely in plastic wrap, and leave it in the fridge until the next day.
♥ Now the fondant is ready to use. Take it out of the fridge a few hours before you want to use it, so that it can reach room temperature. Knead it well before rolling it out. If it's still a bit sticky, knead it in a little powdered sugar.

Chocolate paste

The ratio for this material is two parts chocolate to one part treacle, if you want to scale the recipe up or down. The recipe comes from the cake store Cacas.

You need:

1 lb (500 g) chocolate

½ lb (250 g) light treacle

optionally, a little marzipan

Here's what you do:

- ♥ Carefully melt the chocolate in a water bath.
- ♥ Warm the treacle in a small saucepan until it's lukewarm.
- ♥ Stir the treacle into the melted chocolate. Blend together well.
- ♥ Pour the mixture into a freezer bag. Pat the bag flat and push out all the air. Close the bag tightly and let it sit on the counter for about a day to firm up.
- ♥ Before using the chocolate paste, you have to knead it well. You'll find that it's now rather stiff and hard, but it'll get softer as you knead.
- ♥ If you find that it's a bit difficult to work with, you can knead in a little marzipan to make it smoother.
- ♥ Remember that this chocolate paste will melt if exposed to too much heat, since it's mostly made of chocolate.

Modeling paste

This material is great to use for making decorations like flowers, bows, and other similar things, since it stiffens. I've used this for, among other things, the handle on the coffee cup (page 108) and the purse (page 102), the wings on the bee (page 82) and the ribbons on the present (page 106).

You need:

2 tsp powdered gelatin

6 tsp cold water

3 tsp tragacanth or CMC

about 1 lb (about 500 g) powdered sugar

2 tsp light treacle or glucose

0.5 oz (10 g) hardened coconut oil

1 egg white

Here's what you do:

- ♥ Sprinkle the powdered gelatin in a small saucepan and cover it with water. Let it sit for 5 minutes.
- ♥ Put the tragacanth or CMC and powdered sugar in a stand mixer with a kneading hook. Save a bit of the powdered sugar to adjust the consistency of the substance.
- ♥ Put the saucepan containing the gelatin on a burner and heat it up—but don't let it boil. Stir until the gelatin has dissolved. Add the treacle and coconut butter, and stir until the coconut butter has melted.
- ♥ Add the liquid and egg white to the stand mixer, and let it be kneaded until everything is thoroughly mixed.
- ♥ Pack the substance thoroughly in plastic wrap, and leave it in the fridge until the next day.
- ♥ Now the paste is ready to use. Take it out of the fridge a few hours before you want to use it so that it can reach room temperature. Knead it well before using it.
- ♥ Color the paste with color paste.

BIRTHDAY CAKES

Daisy-shaped Form

You need:

GELATIN TOPPING
1 package flavored gelatin

FILLING
1 package lemon gelatin
½ lb (250 g) plain cream cheese
¼ lb (100 g) powdered sugar
2 tsp vanilla sugar
1 cup (250 mL) light sour cream
1 cup (250 mL) cream

CAKE BASE
½ lb (250 g) digestive biscuits
¼ lb (100 g) margarine/butter

TIPS

You can use two kinds of jelly to get different colors or flavors. You will have jelly to spare, which you can serve with custard in a bowl.

CHEESECAKE WITH GELATIN TOPPING

This is a delightful, fresh cheesecake with a gelatin top.

Here's what you do:

GELATIN TOPPING
- ♥ Prepare the gelatin in two bowls, according to the instructions on the package.
- ♥ Place the bowls in the fridge. After 30 minutes, the smaller of the two portions of gelatin will begin to firm up. Place it in the middle of a daisy pan. Place the pan in the fridge.
- ♥ When the center of the flower is completely firm, carefully pour the rest of the gelatin into the pan. It will have begun to firm up a bit, which is good. Distribute it evenly throughout the petals in the pan.
- ♥ Place the daisy pan back in the fridge. When the gelatin is completely firm, you can start on the filling.

FILLING
- ♥ Prepare the gelatin, but use only half the amount of water.
- ♥ Let the gelatin cool a bit, without becoming firm.
- ♥ Mix the cream cheese, powdered sugar, vanilla sugar, and light sour cream in a stand mixer. Make sure to remove all the lumps.
- ♥ Whip the cream, then mix the whipped cream into the cheese mixture.
- ♥ Add the gelatin; mix well.
- ♥ Distribute the cheese mixture over the gelatin in the daisy pan, and place it in the fridge for about 1 hour.
- ♥ When the cheese mixture has become firm, you can start on the biscuit base.

CAKE BASE
- ♥ Crush the biscuits.
- ♥ Melt the margarine/butter, and mix it with the biscuits.
- ♥ Distribute the biscuit base over the cake in the daisy pan. Use a tablespoon to press it carefully down, while spreading it so that it's smooth and even.
- ♥ Let the cake sit in the fridge for an hour so that the base firms up.
- ♥ Find a dish large enough to accommodate the diameter of the cake. Here's where the cake gets flipped over.
- ♥ Dip the cake pan into warm water for a few seconds so that the gelatin loosens up from the sides. Be careful to avoid getting water on the cake. Then, place the dish upside-down on the pan and flip it over. Carefully take off the cake pan.
- ♥ It's important that you not hold the gelatin in the warm water for too long, or it will begin to melt. If the gelatin remains stuck in the pan, try dipping it for just a couple more seconds so that it lets go.

DELUXE CARROT CAKE

This is a lovely carrot cake with an exotic touch.
The cake should be left to sit a while before serving,
so make it the day before if you can.

You need:

CAKE BASE

1 cup (250 mL) pineapple,
finely diced

3¼ cups (900 mL) carrots,
finely shredded

¾ lb (325 g) wheat flour

3 tsp baking powder

2 tsp baking soda

1 tsp salt

2 tsp cinnamon

½ tsp nutmeg

2 tsp vanilla sugar

½ lb (225 g) margarine/
butter, at room temperature

¾ lb (325 g) sugar

4 eggs

½ cup (125 mL) milk

FILLING

½ lb (225 g) margarine/
butter, at room temperature

3.5 tbsp (50 mL) sour cream
or plain yoghurt

1 lb (500 g) plain cream
cheese

¾ lb (325 g) powdered sugar

1 tsp vanilla sugar

1 cup (250 mL) shredded
coconut

Here's what you do:

CAKE BASE

♥ Heat the oven to 350°F (175°C).
♥ Grease two cake pans, 8 in (20 cm) in diameter, and line them with parchment paper.
♥ Place the finely diced pineapple into a sieve, and press out as much juice as possible with a spoon.
♥ Place the flour in a large bowl. Add the baking powder, baking soda, salt, cinnamon, nutmeg, and vanilla sugar. Blend everything together thoroughly.
♥ Beat the room temperature margarine/butter in a stand mixer until it reaches a creamy consistency. Add in the sugar slowly, and beat the mixture for an additional three minutes.
♥ Beat in the eggs, one at a time.
♥ Next, add in the flour mixture and the milk alternately. The batter should thicken.
♥ Add the shredded carrots and pineapple; mix thoroughly together.
♥ Distribute the batter evenly in both cake pans.
♥ Bake the cakes for 40–45 minutes.
♥ Let the cakes cool completely on a rack.

FILLING

♥ Place the margarine/butter in a stand mixer, and let the mixer run until the margarine/butter is creamed.
♥ Mix in the sour cream or yoghurt.
♥ Then add the cream cheese, but don't mix it for too long, which could cause the cream to become too thin.
♥ Add the powdered sugar and vanilla sugar, then let the mixer run on a low speed until they're thoroughly blended into the mixture. Adjust with sour cream or powdered sugar, should the mixture become too thick or too thin.
♥ Reserve about a quarter of the mixture for the top of the cake.
♥ Blend the shredded coconut into the remaining filling.

DECORATION

♥ Cut each cake in half horizontally, such that you end up with four cake bases.
♥ Distribute the coconut crème in between the cake layers.
♥ Top the cake with the rest of the crème.

CHOCO-STRAWBERRY

This is a dark chocolate cake filled and covered with strawberry crème. On top, a bit of dark ganache. It's decorated with fresh strawberries.

You need:

CAKE BASE
6 oz (175 g) wheat flour

10 oz (275 g) sugar

2.5 oz (75 g) cocoa powder

3 tsp vanilla sugar

1¼ tsp baking soda

1¼ tsp baking powder

5 tbsp (75 mL) rapeseed oil

5 fl oz (150 mL) buttermilk

6¾ tbsp (100 mL) strong coffee

2 eggs

FILLING
a handful of fresh strawberries, or more if you'd like more strawberry flavor

5 egg whites

9 oz (250 g) sugar

1 lb (450 g) margarine/butter, at room temperature

2 tsp vanilla sugar

a bit of pink fondant, to bring out the color

DECORATION
¼ lb (125 g) chocolate

2.5 oz (75 g) margarine/butter

8 fresh, whole strawberries

¼ lb (100 g) chocolate, melted for dipping the strawberries in

Here's what you do:

CAKE BASE
♥ Heat the oven to 350°F (175°C).
♥ Butter two cake pans, 8 in (20 cm) in diameter, and line them with parchment paper.
♥ Blend together all the dry ingredients.
♥ Add the remaining ingredients, and thoroughly mix with a stand mixer.
♥ Beat until everything is well mixed, then distribute evenly in the two cake pans.
♥ Bake the cakes for 30–40 minutes.
♥ Let the cakes cool on a rack.

FILLING
♥ Blend the frozen strawberries into a purée; set them aside.
♥ Place the egg whites and sugar into a metal bowl. Place the bowl over a saucepan containing boiling water. Make sure the bowl doesn't actually touch the water.
♥ Whisk the egg whites and sugar without stopping until they reach a temperature of 150°F (65°C). Measure with a sugar thermometer.
♥ Move the mixture to a stand mixer, and beat on medium speed until the mixture has cooled completely and has doubled in volume.
♥ Stir in the margarine/butter, a bit at a time. Check to see that all of it has been mixed in before adding more. Don't worry if the mixture is a bit lumpy or grainy; it'll continue to change gradually. Continue stirring until the lumps are gone.
♥ Add the vanilla sugar; continue to beat on low speed.
♥ Add the strawberry purée; run the stand mixer until everything is thoroughly incorporated.

DECORATION
♥ Place the chocolate and margarine/butter in a saucepan; melt over low heat. Let the chocolate topping cool a bit and set it to the side.
♥ Melt the dark chocolate. Dip the bottom half of each strawberry in the chocolate. Let the excess chocolate run off, then place them on a piece of parchment paper.
♥ Slice each cake in half horizontally, so you end up with four cake bases.
♥ Spread a thin layer of the crème on each cake base, then put them together. Make sure you have enough crème left to cover the top and sides.
♥ Cover the cake with the rest of the crème using a spatula. If you leave the spatula under running warm water, then dry it off, it'll be easier to spread the crème evenly. That'll make for a nice, smooth result.
♥ Pour the cooled chocolate topping over the cake. It should still be a bit liquid. Spread it smoothly over the top and allow it to drip down the sides some.
♥ Garnish with the fresh strawberries dipped in chocolate.

GRANDMOTHER'S FAVORITE

I'd eat this cake every summer at my grandmother's house, and it's absolutely one of my very favorites. It's kept in the freezer and tastes best when chilled. Here, I've made the cake a bit larger than usual, so that it has two layers.

You need:

CAKE BASE
½ lb (225 g) almonds

½ lb (225 g) powdered sugar

6 egg whites

FILLING
6 egg yolks

5 fl oz (150 mL) whipping cream

7 oz (200 g) sugar

1½ tsp vanilla sugar

½ lb (225 g) margarine/butter, at room temperature

FROSTING
3.5 tbsp (50 mL) whipping cream

2.5 oz (75 g) cooking chocolate, in pieces

½ oz (15 g) margarine/butter

DECORATION
6¾ tbsp (100 mL) whipping cream

½ tsp powdered sugar

Here's what you do:

CAKE BASE
♥ Heat the oven to 320°F (160°C).
♥ Butter three cake pans, 8 in (20 cm) in diameter, and line them with parchment paper.
♥ Grind the almonds and mix them with the powdered sugar.
♥ Beat the egg whites until stiff.
♥ Carefully fold the almond mixture into the egg whites with a rubber spatula.
♥ Distribute the batter thinly on the bottom of each cake pan.
♥ Bake the cake bases in the middle of the oven for 15–20 minutes.
♥ Cool on a rack.

FILLING
♥ Place the egg yolks, cream, and sugar in a saucepan.
♥ Boil while stirring constantly; allow to boil until thick.
♥ Allow the crème to cool a bit.
♥ Stir in the margarine/butter.

FROSTING
♥ Place the cream in a small saucepan, and warm to the boiling point, then remove the saucepan from the heat.
♥ Put in the cooking chocolate and margarine/butter. Stir until the chocolate and margarine/butter have melted.
♥ Stir together thoroughly, so you have a smooth, fine crème.
♥ Place the crème in the fridge until it thickens.

DECORATION
♥ Smooth half the filling over one cake base.
♥ Place the second base on top, and smooth the remaining filling on it.
♥ Place the last base on top of that.
♥ Cover the cake with the frosting.
♥ Place the cake in the freezer.
♥ Take out the cake about 30 minutes before serving it.
♥ Whisk the cream and powdered sugar into a crème. Fill a pastry bag with it.
♥ Create a decorative border around the cake before serving it.

FUDGE CRÈME CAKE

Buttermilk gives cakes a delicious flavor, and a few extra egg yolks give this cake a golden color.

You need:

CAKE BASE
4 eggs

2 egg yolks

1¼ cups (300 mL) buttermilk

¾ lb (350 g) wheat flour

14 oz (400 g) sugar

4 tsp baking powder

3 tsp vanilla sugar

½ lb (225 g) margarine/ butter, at room temperature

FILLING
1⅔ lb (750 g) powdered sugar

¾ lb (350 g) margarine/ butter, at room temperature

6 tbsp cream

3 tsp vanilla sugar

7 oz (200 g) dark cooking chocolate, melted and cooled

DECORATION
cake sprinkles

Here's what you do:

CAKE BASE
- ♥ Heat the oven to 350°F (175°C).
- ♥ Grease two cake pans, 8 inches (20 cm) in diameter, and line the bottoms with parchment paper.
- ♥ Put the eggs, egg yolks, and 2/5 cup (100 mL) of the buttermilk in a mixing bowl; beat until everything's well mixed.
- ♥ Mix the flour, sugar, baking powder, and vanilla sugar in a stand mixer.
- ♥ Put the margarine/butter and the rest of the buttermilk in the flour mixture; blend together thoroughly. Turn up the speed on the stand mixer and beat it until the mixture is light and airy.
- ♥ Add the egg mixture in three parts. Beat thoroughly after each part.
- ♥ Distribute the batter evenly in the two cake pans; bake for 35–45 minutes.
- ♥ Let the cake bases cool on a rack.

FILLING
- ♥ Beat the powdered sugar and margarine/butter together in a stand mixer.
- ♥ Add the other ingredients, and beat for a good while until you have a fluffy crème.

DECORATION
- ♥ Cut the cake bases in two horizontally so you end up with four bases.
- ♥ Place one base on a cake dish and spread a thin layer of crème evenly over the cake. Then add the next base on top and spread a thin layer of crème on it, too. Repeat once more. Place the final base on top, and press carefully down.
- ♥ Cover the top and sides with the crème, but save a bit for decorating after.
- ♥ Fill a piping bag with the remaining crème and make peaks with it on top of the cake. I used piping tip 21 from Wilton here.
- ♥ Scatter colorful sprinkles on top of the cake.
- ♥ The following spread shows how to decorate this cake step by step. In the pictures, I used two cake bases without cutting them; you can choose for yourself if you'd like two thick layers or four thin ones.

➤ ➤ ➤

RAINBOW CAKE

This is a decorative, colorful cake everyone will love.
The surprise comes when you slice the cake . . .

You need:

CAKE BASE

½ lb (225 g) margarine/
butter, at room temperature

1 lb (450 g) sugar

5 egg whites

13 oz (375 g) wheat flour

4 tsp baking powder

2 tsp vanilla sugar

1½ cups (350 mL) milk

red, orange, yellow, green,
blue, and purple color
pastes

FILLING

9 egg whites

¾ lb (350 g) sugar

1 lb (450 g) margarine/
butter, at room temperature

2 tsp lemon extract

a bit of purple color paste

Here's what you do:

CAKE BASE

- ♥ Heat the oven to 350°F (175°C).
- ♥ Grease two or three cake pans, 8 inches (20 cm) in diameter, and line the bottoms with parchment paper.
- ♥ Beat the margarine/butter and sugar until white.
- ♥ Beat in one egg white at a time; beat well in between each one.
- ♥ Blend the flour, baking powder, and vanilla sugar; alternate adding the dry ingredients and the milk. Mix well.
- ♥ Distribute the batter evenly in six bowls. Add an appropriate amount of a different color paste to each bowl and mix.
- ♥ Bake the different colors individually in 8-inch (20-centimeter) cake pans. You'll need to bake the cakes in several rounds. The batter can sit on the counter while the first cake bases are baking.
- ♥ Let each layer bake for about 15 minutes. Check if the cake is ready with a toothpick or skewer. If it comes out dry, the cake is ready.
- ♥ Let the cakes cool on a rack.

FILLING

- ♥ Put the egg whites and sugar in a metal bowl. Place the bowl over a saucepan with boiling water, and make sure the bowl doesn't touch the water.
- ♥ Beat the egg whites and sugar continuously until their temperature reaches 150°F (65°C). Measure with a sugar thermometer.
- ♥ Put the mixture in a stand mixer and beat on medium speed until the mixture is completely cooled off and has doubled in volume.
- ♥ Beat in the margarine/butter, a bit at a time. Make sure everything's thoroughly blended before adding more. Don't worry if the mixture gets a bit lumpy or grainy; it'll gradually change. Continue mixing until the lumps are gone.
- ♥ Add the lemon extract and turn the mixer up to high speed again; beat for about 5 minutes.
- ♥ Finally, add a little color paste and mix until the color has blended with the crème.

Here's how to decorate the rainbow cake

♥ Spread a thin layer of the crème between each layer.

♥ Spread a very thin layer of the crème around and on top of the cake.

♥ Put the cake in the refrigerator so the crème sets and holds on to any crumbs before decorating.

♥ Spread a smooth layer of crème on top of the cake.

♥ Fill a piping bag with the crème and use tip 1A from Wilton, or another similar tip.

♥ Pipe five dots vertically down the side of the cake.

♥ Use a spoon to drag the dots towards the right.

♥ Add a new set of dots along side the one you've just dragged out with the spoon, so that they overlap.

♥ Continue in this manner around the entire cake.

RASPBERRY MERINGUE

The combination of a crisp meringue base covered with a thin layer of chocolate crème, whipped cream, and fresh raspberries is to die for. This is my favorite!

You need:

CAKE BASE

3 egg whites

6 oz (175 g) sugar

1 tsp corn starch

2 oz (50 g) dark chocolate, shaved

CHOCOLATE CRÈME FILLING

5 tbsp (75 mL) cream

⅓ lb (150 g) dark chocolate

CRÈME FILLING

2 cups cream

2 tsp vanilla sugar

¾ lb (350 g) fresh raspberries

Here's what you do:

CAKE BASE

♥ Draw three rectangles, 4 in by 10 in (10 cm by 25 cm) on parchment paper, and place the parchment paper on a baking sheet. There's enough room for three such rectangles.

♥ Heat the oven to 285°F (140°C).

♥ Beat the egg whites until they're stiff and can stand on their own.

♥ Gradually beat in half of the sugar, and continue to beat it until the meringue is stiff and shiny.

♥ Carefully fold in the rest of the sugar, corn starch, and chocolate with a metal spoon.

♥ Place the meringue in a piping bag with an opening of about ½ inch (1 cm). Pipe out stripes across the parchment paper rectangles.

♥ Bake the meringue in the middle of the oven for 1½ hours.

♥ Turn off the oven, but let the meringue sit inside until it's cooled off. Don't open the oven door.

♥ Carefully remove the parchment paper from the meringue.

CHOCOLATE CRÈME FILLING

♥ Put the cream in a saucepan and bring it to a boil. Take the pan off the flame and add the chocolate. Stir until the chocolate has melted. Let the crème cool until it's a bit thicker.

CRÈME FILLING

♥ Beat the cream and vanilla sugar into a crème.

DECORATION

♥ Spread a thin layer of chocolate crème on each meringue base. Make sure there isn't too much, as the meringue base can quickly break.

♥ Place one base on a cake dish and pipe the crème on it in a decorative manner. Distribute one third of the raspberries evenly over the crème.

♥ Place the next base carefully on the raspberries, and repeat the process with the crème and raspberries. Remember that it's easy to break the meringue base, so be careful when you place them on top of each other.

♥ Carefully place the final base on top and repeat the process with the crème and raspberries.

BIRTHDAY LAYER CAKE WITH STRAWBERRIES

A layer cake that's not covered on the sides is often called a "naked cake." The cake looks tempting when you see that it's filled with lots of tasty strawberry pieces.

You need:

CAKE BASE

5 eggs

⅓ lb (150 g) sugar

⅓ lb (150 g) wheat flour

¾ tsp baking powder

FILLING AND DECORATION

2½ cups cream

3 tsp powdered sugar

2 baskets of strawberries

1 basket of blueberries

Here's what you do:

CAKE BASE

♥ Heat the oven to 350°F (175°C).

♥ Grease a cake pan, 8 in (20 cm) in diameter, and line the bottom with parchment paper.

♥ Beat the eggs and sugar until white and fluffy. You should be able to turn the bowl upside down without the egg mixture coming out.

♥ Sift the flour and baking powder into the egg mixture so that the cake doesn't have lumps in it.

♥ Carefully fold the dry ingredients into the egg mixture with a wooden spoon.

♥ Pour the batter into the pan. Place it straight into the oven; sponge cakes can't tolerate being left out before baking. That causes the cake to collapse.

♥ Bake the cake on the lowest shelf in the oven for about 30 minutes. The cake should be golden and is ready when it lets go of the pan. You might like to use a toothpick or skewer to check whether the cake is ready.

♥ Let the cake cool on a rack.

FILLING AND DECORATION

♥ Slice the strawberries into pieces, but save a few to decorate the top.

♥ Whip the cream and powdered sugar until stiff.

♥ Slice the sponge cake into three layers. Place one of the layers on a dish.

♥ Moisten the three bases with a bit of milk.

♥ Put one third of the crème on the cake base and place half of the strawberry pieces on the crème. Make sure they reach the edges, too, so that they're visible after you put the next layer on top. Repeat.

♥ Finally, spread the rest of the crème on the top of the cake only, and decorate it with strawberries and blueberries.

CHOCOLATE SURPRISE

This is a German-inspired cake with tart jam, cream, and chocolate. It looks like a normal layer cake, but the chocolate surprise comes when you slice it.

You need:

CAKE BASE

1 cup (250 mL) milk

2 oz (50 g) cocoa powder

3.5 oz (100 g) sugar

3.5 oz (100 g) margarine/ butter, at room temperature

⅓ lb (150 g) sugar

4 tsp vanilla sugar

2 eggs

6 oz (175 g) wheat flour

1½ tsp baking powder

FILLING AND DECORATION

2.5 cups (600 mL) cream

3 tsp powdered sugar

100 g chocolate

about 7 oz (about 200 g) apricot jelly

Here's what you do:

CAKE BASE

♥ Heat the oven to 350°F (175°C).

♥ Grease two baking pans, 8 inches (20 cm) in diameter, and line the bottoms with parchment paper.

♥ Mix the milk, cocoa powder, and sugar. Boil while stirring, and let cool.

♥ Beat the margarine/butter, sugar, and vanilla sugar together in a stand mixer.

♥ Add the eggs, one at a time. Beat each one in thoroughly before adding the next one.

♥ Mix the flour and baking powder, and alternately mix in this and the cooled cocoa.

♥ Pour the batter into the pans.

♥ Bake the cakes on a low rack in the oven for 20–30 minutes.

♥ Let the cakes sit for a few minutes in their pans before you turn them out onto a rack.

♥ Let the cakes cool, and slice each in half so that you have four bases.

FILLING AND DECORATION

♥ Whip the cream and powdered sugar together until stiff.

♥ Grate or shave the chocolate.

♥ Spread a layer of jelly on the lowest base, and then a layer of the stiff crème. Place the next base on top, and then more jelly and crème. Repeat with the third cake base.

♥ Place the final base on top and press carefully down.

♥ Cover the cake with a thin layer of crème on the top and sides. Use a Wilton #21 piping tip (or equivalent) and pipe it around the edge of the cake. Sprinkle the chocolate liberally on top.

♥ Let the cake sit for a few hours in the fridge before serving it, which will help to make it more moist.

♥ Decorate with colorful birthday candles.

RICH CHOCOLATE CAKE

This is a strong chocolate cake for all the chocolate lovers out there, so you only need to cover the cake with the crème, with no filling. Decorate with colorful cake pops.

You need:

CAKE BASE

½ lb (250 g) cooking chocolate

3.5 oz (100 g) margarine/butter

6 egg yolks

2.5 oz (75 g) sugar

100 g ground almonds

6 egg whites

CRÈME:

7 oz (200 g) cooking chocolate

2 oz (50 g) margarine/butter

5 fl oz (150 mL) cream

Here's what you do:

CAKE BASE

♥ Heat the oven to 350°F (175°C).

♥ Grease a baking pan 9.5 inches (24 cm) in diameter, and line the bottom with parchment paper.

♥ Melt the chocolate and margarine/butter in a microwave oven or hot water bath.

♥ Beat the egg yolks and sugar together.

♥ Add the ground almonds and the melted chocolate mixture.

♥ Beat the egg whites until stiff, and fold them into the batter.

♥ Bake the cake for about 45 minutes.

♥ Let it cool on a rack.

CRÈME:

♥ Place the chocolate, margarine/butter, and cream in a bowl. Melt everything together over a water bath or in a microwave oven.

♥ Stir everything together into a crème.

♥ Let the crème cool until spreadable.

♥ Spread the crème over and around the chocolate cake.

Cake pops

There are two ways to make cake pops—either using leftover cake or by baking small, round balls of batter in a silicon mold or an iron made for this purpose.

If you choose to make them out of leftover cake, melt a sheet of chocolate in the oven or over a water bath and mix it with the leftover cake to form a dough. Roll small balls of this dough, about the size of ping-pong balls.

If you'd like to bake the cake pops in a mold or iron, you can use the recipe on the next page, which is enough for 32 pieces. For this cake, you need 8 cake pops. You can put the ones you don't use in the freezer to use later.

♥ ♥ ♥

You need:

CAKE POPS (32 PIECES)

1 egg

6 oz (175 g) sugar

⅓ lb (150 g) wheat flour

1 oz (25 g) cocoa powder

1½ tsp baking powder

1½ tsp vanilla sugar

5 fl oz (150 mL) milk

2 oz (50 g) melted margarine/butter

1 ripe banana, mashed

DECORATION (8 PIECES)

3.5 oz (100 g) white chocolate

about ½ tbsp rapeseed oil or melted coconut fat

a bit of blue coloring paste

4 lollipop sticks, 6 inches (15 cm)

green, white, and blue cake sprinkles

Cake Pops

Here's what you do:

CAKE POPS

♥ Heat the oven to 350°F (175°C).

♥ Brush the pan with a bit of margarine/butter.

♥ Beat the eggs and sugar together.

♥ Mix the dry ingredients and alternately add them and the milk to the egg mixture, whisking the entire time.

♥ Add the melted margarine/butter and mix well.

♥ Finally, add in the mashed banana; mix thoroughly.

♥ Fill the pan completely and put on the lid.

♥ Bake the cake pops in the middle of the oven for 15–20 minutes.

♥ Let them cool on a rack.

DECORATION

♥ Melt the white chocolate in a microwave oven or over a water bath. Remember that white chocolate doesn't tolerate as much heat as regular chocolate and can burn easily. Stir it around so that all of the chocolate is melted evenly, without lumps.

♥ Add the oil or fat to thin out the chocolate a bit. This is necessary to get a good result when you dip the cake pops in chocolate. Add a bit of color paste and stir until everything is evenly mixed.

♥ Cut the lollipop sticks in half, so that they aren't so ridiculously tall compared to the cake.

♥ Dip the ends of the sticks in a bit of the chocolate and push them into the cake pops. Place them in the fridge for about 15 minutes, until the chocolate has firmed up and the sticks are well-attached to the cake pops.

♥ Place the melted chocolate in a small cup, which will make it easier to cover the cake pops in chocolate. (If the chocolate's begun to harden, place it in the microwave for 10 seconds.) Dip the cake pop into the chocolate, making sure to cover it completely. Lift it up, and let the excess chocolate come off before setting it in a sugar-filled glass, in Styrofoam, or in a cake pop stand for storage.

♥ Before the chocolate on the cake pops has solidified completely, sprinkle the cake sprinkles onto them. If you wait until the chocolate is firm, the sprinkles won't stay on the chocolate. Should this happen, I'd recommend simply dipping the cake pops in the chocolate again.

♥ Place the cake pops in the fridge for half an hour before using them to decorate the cake.

BANANA CAKE WITH CREAM CHEESE

This cake is delicious, but also strong because of the element of cheesecake. You've got to like bananas to like this cake.

You need:

CAKE BASE,
BANANA CAKE

3.5 oz (100 g) margarine/
butter, melted

3 eggs

7 oz (200 g) sugar

$1/_3$ lb (150 g) wheat flour

1 tsp baking powder

$2/_3$ lb (300 g) ripe banana,
mashed

3.5 oz (100 g) dark chocolate,
chopped

CAKE BASE,
BANANA CHEESECAKE

14 oz (400 g) cream cheese

2 oz (50 g) powdered sugar

2 oz (50 g) sugar

2 tsp vanilla sugar

2 eggs

6 oz (175 g) ripe banana,
mashed

You need:

CAKE BASE, BANANA CAKE
- ♥ Heat the oven to 350°F (175°C).
- ♥ Grease two baking pans, 8 inches (20 cm) in diameter, and line the bottoms with parchment paper.
- ♥ Melt the margarine/butter in a saucepan.
- ♥ Beat the eggs and sugar together.
- ♥ Sift the flour and baking powder into the egg mixture and add the melted margarine/butter. Whisk until there aren't any clumps left in the batter.
- ♥ Lastly, mix in the mashed banana and chopped chocolate. Use a stand mixer to mix it thoroughly.
- ♥ Bake the cakes in the middle of the oven for 20–30 minutes.
- ♥ Let the cakes cool a bit before taking them out of their pans. Let them cool completely on a rack.

CAKE BASE, BANANA CHEESECAKE
- ♥ Heat the oven to 480°F (250°C).
- ♥ Grease a baking pan, 8 inches (20 cm) in diameter, and line the bottom with parchment paper.
- ♥ Place the cream cheese in a bowl, and stir it for a few minutes until it's airy.
- ♥ Add the powdered sugar, sugar, and vanilla sugar, and stir until it's all well mixed.
- ♥ Add one egg at a time; stir until well mixed.
- ♥ Lastly, add in the mashed banana, and stir well.
- ♥ Pour the batter into the pan.
- ♥ Bake the cake for 10 minutes at 480°F (250°C). Then, turn the oven down to 250°F (120°C), and prop open the oven door for about 10 minutes, which will lower the temperature in the oven from 480°F (250°C) to 250°F (120°C). Bake the cake for an additional 50 minutes.
- ♥ Let the cake cool on a rack.

BANANA CRÈME:

5 egg whites

¾ lb (350 g) sugar

1 lb (450 g) margarine/
butter, at room temperature

2 tsp vanilla sugar

¼ lb (125 g) ripe banana,
mashed

a bit of yellow coloring
paste

DECORATION

3.5 oz (100 g) chocolate
chips

⅖ cup (100 mL) cream

½ tsp powdered sugar

a bit of melted chocolate
or chocolate sauce

cake sprinkles

8 maraschino cherries

BANANA CRÈME:

♥ Place the egg whites and sugar in a metal bowl. Put the bowl over a saucepan with boiling water inside, and make sure the bowl doesn't come into contact with the water.

♥ Beat the egg whites and sugar without stopping until they reach a temperature of 150°F (65°C). Measure with a sugar thermometer.

♥ Then, put the egg whites in a stand mixer and beat on medium speed until the mixture is completely cooled and has doubled in size.

♥ Stir in the margarine/butter, a bit at a time. Make sure everything is thoroughly mixed before adding more. Don't worry if the mixture is a bit lumpy or grainy. This will gradually change. Continue stirring until all the lumps are gone.

♥ Add the vanilla sugar and mashed banana, and stir until well mixed.

♥ Add a bit of yellow coloring paste to obtain a light-yellow crème.

DECORATION

♥ Place the banana cake on a cake dish, and spread a thin layer of the banana crème over it. Sprinkle half the chocolate chips over the crème.

♥ Place the banana cheesecake on top, and spread another layer of the banana crème over it. Sprinkle on the rest of the chocolate chips.

♥ Finally, place the second banana cake on top and press it carefully down.

♥ Distribute the rest of the banana crème on the top and sides. You can smooth out the crème or play around with the spatula a bit, so that you get some waves and motion in the crème. You can also make stripes around the side with a decorating triangle.

♥ Whip the cream and powdered sugar to make a crème. Fill a piping bag with it.

♥ Pipe peaks of the crème around the top of the cake with the same distance between them all. Pipe a little melted chocolate or chocolate sauce over the peaks, back and forth. Nothing's wrong with a little chocolate running down the sides, should that happen.

♥ Sprinkle over colorful cake sprinkles up to the edge of the crème.

♥ To finish, carefully place a maraschino cherry on each crème peak around the cake.

SCHÖNBRUNNER TORTE

This is a variant of a delicious chocolate and nut cake, which is named after what once was an imperial palace near Vienna.

You need:

CAKE BASE

3.5 oz (100 g) dark cooking chocolate

7 oz (200 g) margarine/butter

7 oz (200 g) powdered sugar

6 egg yolks

2.5 oz (75 g) wheat flour

⅓ lb (150 g) ground almonds

6 egg whites

1 pinch of salt

FILLING AND DECORATION

3.5 oz (100 g) hazelnuts

2 oz (50 g) corn starch

2 cups (500 mL) milk

3.5 oz (100 g) milk chocolate

6 oz (175 g) margarine/butter

3.5 oz (100 g) powdered sugar

Here's what you do:

CAKE BASE:

♥ Heat the oven to 390°F (200°C).

♥ Grease a baking pan, 9.5 inches (24 cm) in diameter, and line the bottom with parchment paper.

♥ Melt the chocolate over a water bath or in a microwave oven.

♥ Beat the margarine/butter, powdered sugar, and egg yolks to form a light, airy crème.

♥ Stir in the melted chocolate.

♥ Sift the wheat flour and almond flour together, and mix this into the batter.

♥ Whisk the egg whites until stiff with the salt, and fold this carefully into the batter.

♥ Bake the cake on the lowest rack in the oven for about 50 minutes.

♥ Let the cake cool on a rack.

FILLING AND DECORATION

♥ Finely grind the nuts.

♥ Dissolve the corn starch in a bit of the milk.

♥ Warm the rest of the milk in a saucepan and melt the milk chocolate in the milk.

♥ Stir the corn starch mixture into the chocolate milk, and boil it briefly.

♥ Let the chocolate milk cool off completely.

♥ Stir the margarine/butter and powdered sugar to obtain an airy crème.

♥ Mix together the chocolate milk, butter cream, and ground nuts to make a chocolate crème.

♥ Slice the cake into three bases.

♥ Put the bases together with a thin layer of chocolate crème between each one.

♥ Cover the sides and top of the cake with a layer of the crème. Place the remainder in a piping bag with a #1M piping tip from Wilton (or equivalent).

♥ Pipe small rosettes on top of the cake. Make them by holding the piping bag straight up and down, at a 90-degree angle to the cake, and press out a star. Without reducing the pressure on the piping bag, drag it carefully around the star once. Carefully release the pressure as you finish, so that the crème doesn't abruptly stop, but instead glides smoothly into the rosette.

♥ Keep the cake cool until it's ready to be served.

SACHERTORTE

This is a variant of a good, old favorite. Apricot jelly gives it a very fresh taste.

You need:

CAKE BASE

⅓ lb (150 g) dark chocolate

½ vanilla bean

6 eggs

1 pinch salt

¼ lb (125 g) margarine/ butter, at room temperature

3.5 oz (100 g) sugar

¼ lb (125 g) wheat flour

FILLING AND DECORATION

7 oz (200 g) apricot jelly

7 oz (200 g) dark chocolate

1 tbsp neutral oil, e.g. rapeseed

Here's what you do:

CAKE BASE

♥ Heat the oven to 340°F (170°C).
♥ Grease a baking pan, 9.5 inches (24 cm) in diameter, and line the bottom with parchment paper.
♥ Melt the chocolate over a water bath or in a microwave oven. Let it cool until it's warm to the touch.
♥ Slice open the vanilla bean and scrape out the seeds with a spoon.
♥ Separate the egg yolks and egg whites.
♥ Beat the egg whites until stiff with the salt. Make sure all your equipment's clean, or the egg whites won't stiffen.
♥ Beat the margarine/butter, sugar, and vanilla seeds until bright white, so that the sugar is dissolved in. Stir in a bit of the egg yolks at a time, and beat until everything is thoroughly mixed. Lastly, mix in the cooled chocolate.
♥ Fold the stiffly beaten egg whites and wheat flour into the butter mixture.
♥ Bake the cake for about 45 minutes. Turn off the oven and let the cake sit an additional 15 minutes. Then take the cake out of the oven and let it cool a little in its pan before you set it on a rack to cool.

FILLING AND DECORATION

♥ Warm the apricot jelly in a saucepan.
♥ Slice the cake into two bases.
♥ Spread a layer of the jam on the base, and place the top of the cake on it.
♥ Spread the rest of the jelly around and on top of the cake. Let it sit for two hours.
♥ Melt the chocolate over a water bath or in a microwave oven. Stir in the oil, and let the chocolate mixture cool off until warm to the touch.
♥ Set the cake on a piece of parchment paper. Pour the liquid chocolate over it and spread it carefully on the top and sides with a spatula.
♥ Set the cake aside somewhere cool for at least 3 hours before serving.

RED VELVET CAKE

This is a typical American cake that's colored red. It's often made with cream cheese; here, we use both cream cheese and mascarpone.

You need:

CAKE BASE
¼ lb (125 g) margarine/butter, at room temperature

⅔ lb (300 g) sugar

2 eggs

3 tsp cocoa powder

½ lb (250 g) wheat flour

2 tsp vanilla sugar

4–6 tsp red coloring paste

1 cup (250 mL) buttermilk

1 tsp baking soda

1 tsp white wine vinegar

FILLING
½ lb (225 g) plain cream cheese

½ lb (225 g) mascarpone

2 tsp vanilla sugar

¼ lb (125 g) powdered sugar

1½ cups (350 mL) cream

DECORATION
red sugar pearls

Here's what you do:

CAKE BASE
♥ Heat the oven to 350°F (175°C).
♥ Grease two baking pans, 8 inches (20 cm) in diameter, and line the bottoms with parchment paper.
♥ Beat the margarine/butter and sugar until light and airy.
♥ Add the eggs, one at a time; beat them in well.
♥ Sift together the cocoa powder, flour, and vanilla sugar.
♥ Stir the red coloring paste into the buttermilk.
♥ Mix the wet and dry ingredients alternately into the butter mixture, beating it in a stand mixer on medium speed.
♥ Mix the baking powder and white wine vinegar in a small cup. Let the mixture start to bubble, then stir it quickly into the batter.
♥ Working quickly, distribute the batter in the pans. Bake the cakes for 25–30 minutes.
♥ Let the cakes cool on a rack.

FILLING
♥ Stir together the cream cheese and mascarpone to form a smooth crème.
♥ Add the vanilla sugar and powdered sugar, and continue stirring until everything's well mixed and smooth.
♥ Add the cream and beat the mixture until it's thick enough to spread on the cake.

DECORATION
♥ Slice the cakes in two horizontally, so you get four cake bases.
♥ Place the first base on a dish, and spread a layer of butter cream over the whole thing.
♥ Place the next base on top, add the crème, and repeat with the third base.
♥ Place the final base on top, and press carefully down.
♥ Distribute the rest of the crème on the top and sides of the cake.
♥ Decorate with tasty, red sugar pearls on the top and at the bottom, along the edge.

FESTIVE ICE CREAM

Often, you'll find yourself with lots of leftover egg yolks and wondering what to do with them. A good option is homemade ice cream. This ice cream is better than most ice cream you can buy, and you can add just about anything you want to create the flavor you'd like. There are some suggestions in this recipe, but you can add whatever you wish to.

You need:

5 egg yolks

3.5 oz (100 g) sugar

½ vanilla bean

1¼ cups (300 mL) cream

chopped chocolate

Here's what you do:

♥ Beat the egg yolks and sugar together.
♥ Slice the vanilla bean open and scrape out the seeds with a spoon.
♥ Whip the cream until stiff along with the vanilla seeds, and fold this into the egg mixture.
♥ Place the mixture in a small bread pan and set it in the freezer.
♥ Scatter the chopped chocolate over the ice cream before serving it.

TIP

If you'd like a different flavor of ice cream, you can mix in strawberry purée, raspberry purée, mashed bananas, M&Ms, or chocolate milk powder into the cream. Try dividing the ice cream mixture into two or three different containers and making a different flavor in each one.

If you don't have vanilla beans handy, you can also use a little vanilla sugar.

Themed cakes are slightly different cakes, covered and decorated with fondant or marzipan. The possibilities are many; here, your imagination is the only thing that can stop you. Choose whatever basic recipe for a cake and crème you like, and follow its recipe; then, make the themed cake as explained in the recipe here.

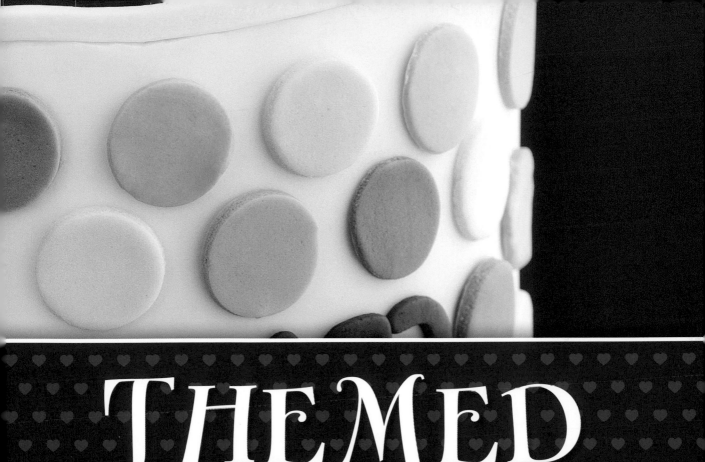

THEMED CAKES

LADYBUG AND BEE CAKE

These cakes are sweet and work well as birthday cakes for the littlest children, both boys and girls.

You need:

a sports ball mold

red, black, and yellow decorating material, plus a bit of white and blue for the eyes

modeling paste to make the wings of the bee

round cutters in different sizes

a modeling tool with a slightly sharp edge or perhaps a knitting needle

a cutting wheel

a sharp knife

edible glue

a brush

parchment paper

spaghetti, for the feelers

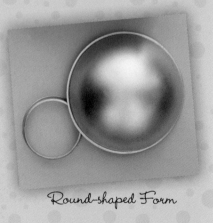

Round-shaped Form

Here's what you do:

♥ Use a sports ball mold; fill both parts with cake dough.

♥ Bake a cake in each of the two molds.

♥ Start by making the wings for the bee in Mexican paste: roll out the dough and cut out two similar wings. Place them aside and let them dry. It's best to make these at least a day in advance.

♥ Fill the cakes and cover them with a thin layer of crème. Don't use too much, which can make the cakes lose their unique shape.

♥ Cover one cake with a yellow top. Roll out the black material and cut it into two or three strips of equal size. Place them on top of the yellow cover. There should be a face on the front of the figure, so place the first strip a bit further towards the middle. Place the cake in the fridge while you continue with the ladybug cake.

♥ Cover this cake with a red top. Carefully mark where the wings are split with a cake tool or knitting needle on top of the ladybug. Start behind the place where the head goes, and continue all the way down.

♥ Cut out black circles, three large and three a bit smaller, which you can glue onto each side of the body.

♥ Next, start on the faces. Make two similar faces, one for the bee and one for the ladybug. Roll two clumps of black material into slightly elliptical balls. Press them somewhat flat. Make the eyes with the white, blue, and black material. Roll balls in different sizes and press them flat; glue them to the faces. Mark the mouths with a tool or knitting needle, and then glue the faces onto the cakes.

♥ Roll four cylinders out for the feelers. Push a piece of spaghetti through each one, and let a little bit of the spaghetti stick out of each side. Fasten the feelers onto the heads by pressing the spaghetti into the heads a bit and placing a little glue where the feelers are fastened. Then, roll four small balls to glue on top of the cylinders where a little bit of spaghetti is sticking out.

♥ Make two cuts on each side of the bee cake where the wings go. Push the wings into the cake. Be careful, as they break easily.

♥ If you have leftover decorating material, you can make some flowers out of them—red and white, blue and white, or yellow and white, to put candles in. Roll out some balls and press them slightly flat, but make sure they're thick, or the candles won't stay in place. Place them around the bee and ladybug on the cake dish, and push a candle into the center of each flower.

HELLO KITTY CAKE

Making character cakes is easier than you might imagine. The same process works for all characters you could wish for; just replace the picture. Characters like Winnie-the-Pooh, dinosaurs, Smurfs, and so on can be made easily in the same way. If you want to make a larger cake out of a long-pan cake, simply print the picture out across two pages, and tape them together.

You need:

a rectangular cake base, baked in a small, long pan

a picture of Hello Kitty

white decorating material to make the cake cover

a bit of red (or other color, for the clothes), black, and orange material for details

a cutting wheel

a sharp knife

a sugar gun

white sugar pearls

edible glue

a brush

Here's what you do:

♥ Print out a picture of Hello Kitty and cut it out. Place it on top of the cake.
♥ Cut around the picture with a sharp knife. Make sure to cut directly down, so you get an even edge around the cake. The leftover pieces of cake are good for making cake pops; you can serve these alongside the cake or put them in the freezer for later use.
♥ Fill the cake and cover it with a thin layer of crème.
♥ Also spread a thin layer of the crème on the sides of the cake, before putting the covering on top.
♥ Roll out a cover a bit larger than the cake, and place it carefully over the cake. Use a cake smoother to stroke the top of the cake, which will let you carefully press the covering on, remove any air bubbles, and get a nice, smooth cover.
♥ At this point, it's important that your hands are completely clean. Slide the material inwards, towards the edge of the cake itself, with your palms. Use your palms as cake smoothers to even out any uneven bits.
♥ Cut away any excess material from the cake with a cutting wheel. Go over the top and sides with a cake smoother to finish.
♥ Cut out the dress from the figure you used to cut out the cake. You'll use the same technique as you would with a jigsaw puzzle: roll out a bit of red material and place the dress on top. Cut around the picture with a cutting wheel. Fasten the dress to the cake. I make the dress first, then place it on the cake. Afterwards, I make the sleeves, and finally the arm nearest us, when looking at the picture from the top down.
♥ Roll two black balls for the eyes, making them slightly elliptical before pressing them flat. Attach the eyes to the cake. Do the same with the nose, for which you'll use the orange material. Roll out two thin cylinders for the whiskers. Cut each one in thirds, and attach the whiskers to the cake. In the picture, you can see how the eyes, nose, and whiskers are placed.
♥ Make a flower to attach to one of the ears in the same color as the dress and with an orange circle in the middle.
♥ Decorate both the dress and flower with the pearls.
♥ Use a sugar gun to make a long, thin, black border to place around the figure at the end. This way, the character is more clearly outlined, and takes on a bit more of a cartoon-style appearance.

PIRATE CAKE

A pirate cake is never amiss at an event for kids. This is a simple, decorative cake with all the most important elements: wooden planks, like on a pirate ship, a pirate boy, and gold coins.

You need:

a round cake base

brown decorating material to cover the cake (preferably fondant with cocoa powder)

flesh tone, black, white, red, and a bit of blue material (for the face impression)

mat or rolling pin with wood pattern

a somewhat large, round cutter and some smaller round cutters

a cutting wheel

edible glue

a brush

chocolate gold coins

Here's what you do:

♥ Fill the cake and cover it with a thin layer of crème.

♥ Roll out the material and cut out a circle as big as the surface of the cake. Use the baking pan as a guide. Cover the top of the cake with the circle. Use a cake smoother to even it out.

♥ Roll out more of the material and cut it into strips. Press a wood pattern into the strips with the help of a mat or rolling pin with such a pattern.

♥ Attach the strips to the cake, one at a time, down the sides.

♥ Take a look at the step-by-step pictures of how to make the pattern on the side of the cake, and the face of the pirate on the next page.

♥ Next, start making the pirate. Cut out a circle of flesh-colored material for the face. Cut out an equally-large red circle, but cut away the lower part of the circle. You should be left with a semicircle, which will be the pirate's bandana. Attach it to the face.

♥ Cut out two leaf-shaped bits and roll a small ball, then press it a bit flat to make the knotted part of the bandana. Press out white circles in two different sizes to attach to the bandana.

♥ Make the pirate's eye from small circles placed on top of each other— first white, then blue and black. Cut out an eye patch.

♥ Glue on the eye and eye patch. Roll a round ball of flesh-colored material to glue on for the nose.

♥ Use a sugar gun to make a thin black line for the mouth and for the cord of the eye patch. Glue in place.

♥ Continue by making a long, black border with the sugar gun to fasten around the entire face and bandana of the pirate. This isn't absolutely necessary, but I think the face comes forward more and gets a bit of a cartoonish look, which improves the design.

♥ Decorate with lots of gold coins around the cake, preferably chocolate ones.

1.

2.

3.

4.

5.

6.

PRINCESS CAKE

Nearly every little girl's dream is to become a princess. A pink cake with tiaras and pearls would certainly be ideal for a little princess.

You need:

modeling paste for the crown

a template or model for the crown that goes on top

a round cutter

plastic wrap and a thermos

two heart-shaped cutters, one small and one large

a round cake, 8 inches (20 cm) in diameter, and another, 6 inches (15 cm) in diameter

wooden sticks and cardboard

pink and white decorating material

a cutting wheel

pink and white sugar pearls, 1/5 inch (4 mm)

tweezers

a diamond-shaped imprint tool

a pearl border mold

a princess crown mold

edible glue

a brush

Here's what you do:

- ♥ Start by making the crown that goes on top of the cake. Make this one day or more in advance.
- ♥ Make a guide out of paper for the crown by drawing five sharp triangles next to each other, joined at their bases. Cut this out. (See the detail photos on the next page.)
- ♥ Roll out the modeling material. Place the guide on top and cut it out.
- ♥ Use a round cutter to cut out a little transition between each triangle in the crown.
- ♥ Cover a thermos or similar object with plastic wrap. What's important is that you have something tall and round, in the right size for you to wrap the crown around when it's drying. Place the crown around the thermos, upside-down, to dry. Make sure the joints and edges are even. If you put the crown on the thermos right-side-up, the tips will fall back and down.
- ♥ Let the crown dry for at least a day.
- ♥ When the crown is dry, glue on hearts in the same color as the cake itself.
- ♥ Fill the cakes and cover them with a thin layer of crème. They'll look best if the cakes are the same height. The smallest cake should rest on a cardboard disc of the exact same diameter as the cake itself. It shouldn't be visible, but should function as a support when the two cakes are stacked.
- ♥ Roll out the pink material and cover both cakes.
- ♥ Place one cake in the fridge while you decorate the other.
- ♥ Start by decorating the lower cake. Place it on a cake dish and cover it with a white pearl border. Fill the pearl mold with the white material and press it down well with the help of a rolling pin. Take a sharp knife and carefully cut away the excess material. Make sure not to accidentally cut the mold itself. Press the pearl border out of the mold and attach it to the cake with some edible glue. If you don't have a mold like this, you can roll small, round balls and glue them together.
- ♥ Make small princess crowns with the help of the small crown mold. Push the white material down into the mold and smooth over it with a rolling pin. Cut away extra material, being careful to avoid cutting the mold itself. Press the crown out. You'll need about eight crowns. Carefully cut away the heart already on the crown, and glue on a small pink heart instead, so that it looks like the crown that goes on top. Fasten these around the cake with the edible glue.
- ♥ Switch over to the other cake. Use a diamond-shaped imprint tool to make the pattern. If you don't have one of these, you can use a ruler

♥ ♥ ♥

and a knitting needle to make lines in the same pattern. Make a small indentation in each place the lines intersect.

♥ Cut three wooden or plastic sticks to push into the larger cake, which sits on the bottom. Place the smaller cake on top. Make sure that the small cake is in the middle of the large cake; preferably, use a ruler to measure. See also 'How to make tiered cakes' on page 18.

♥ Continue to decorate the upper cake. Make a pearl border, as described above, and glue it to the bottom of the cake. Now you've covered the separation between the two cakes.

♥ Use tweezers to pick up white sugar pearls, dip part of them in a bit of edible glue, and attach them in the indentations. Continue around the whole cake.

♥ Finally, set the crown on top. Use a bit of edible glue under the crown to fasten it in place. Glue the pink sugar pearls around the base of the crown. Use the tweezers and glue once more to attach them. You don't have to use tweezers, but I find that they simplify the job, since the pearls are small.

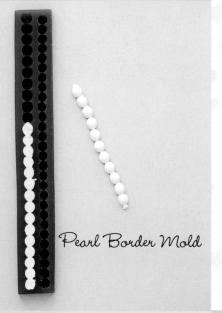

Pearl Border Mold

TIP

You can choose whether you want to decorate each cake individually before assembling them, or to assemble them first and then decorate. If you plan on transporting the cake somewhere else, it's more practical to decorate the cake first and assemble the parts when it's time to serve the cake.

Diamond-shaped Imprint Tool

Heart-shaped Cutters

Crown Top Template

Princess Crown Mold

WINNIE-THE-POOH CAKE

This cake is decorated with a puzzle picture. You can swap out Winnie-the-Pooh for whatever other character you like. I recommend starting with simple figures and moving on to more difficult ones gradually as you get more experience.

You need:

a round cake base

blue decorating material to cover the cake

a cutting wheel

white material for the letters and border around the bottom of the cake

letter-shaped cutters

a pearl border mold

a bit of orange, red, and black material for the actual figure

a hobby knife

a sugar gun, to make a thin black border around the figure

black and red color pens with edible ink

edible glue

a brush

Here's what you do:

♥ Start by making the figure that you'll use to decorate the cake. See how to make this under 'How to make puzzle plaques' on page 20.
♥ Roll out the white material and cut out the letters you'll use to write on the cake. If they can sit for a little while and dry before you lift them, they'll retain their shape better.
♥ Fill a round cake and cover it with a thin layer of crème.
♥ Roll out blue material and cover the cake with it. Place the cake on a dish.
♥ Make a pearl border to glue onto the base of the cake, along the edge. Fill the pearl mold with white material and press it down well with the help of a rolling pin. Take a sharp knife and carefully cut away the excess material. Make sure not to accidentally cut the mold itself. Press the pearl border out of the mold and attach it to the cake with some edible glue. If you don't have such a mold, you can roll small, round balls and glue them together.
♥ Attach the figure to the cake with some edible glue. Make sure to decide where the letters will go first, so you can leave room for them.
♥ Finally, glue on the letters. Try placing them on the cake before gluing them, so that you can see if you're happy with the placement.

Letter-shaped Cutters

MONSTER CAKE

A monster cake can be fun to make for a child's birthday with some scary effects. Lots of children find monsters, aliens, and other such characters exciting, something reflected in many animated children's films. This particular monster is rather friendly.

You need:

two round cake bases with a diameter of 6 inches (15 cm)

half a sports ball cake

green decorating material to cover the cake with

a cutting wheel

a bit of white, blue, and black material for the eye

round cutters for the eye

spaghetti for the antennae

edible glue

a brush

Here's what you do:

♥ Begin by filling the two cake bases with crème. Place them on top of each other. Place the crème on top of the two stacked cakes, and lastly, place the round cake half on top. You can get this round cake half by baking a cake in half a sports ball pan.

♥ Cover the entire cake with a thin layer of crème.

♥ Roll out the green material for a cover, and place it over the cake. Smooth out the top and upper portion of the cake with a cake smoother, but let the rest of the cover simply fall naturally down in fine waves. Cut around the edge at the bottom with a cutting wheel.

♥ Cut out a large circle of white material for the eye. Glue it a good ways up on the cake. Make a new circle of blue material to glue on the white one. Then make a smaller, black circle to glue on the blue one. To finish, you can make a tiny little white circle to glue on the edge between the blue and black parts of the eye. This gives the eye more life. Now you've made a large eye, which you glue on.

♥ Roll out a bit of black material and cut it out in a crescent moon shape for the mouth. Cut out some sharp triangles in white material for the teeth. Glue them on the mouth. Glue the mouth on beneath the eye.

♥ Roll out two cylinders for the antennae in the same color as the body. Push a piece of spaghetti through them to make them stiff. Let a bit of spaghetti stick out on both sides. Attach the antennae by pushing the spaghetti pieces into the head. Use a bit of edible glue where they're attached. Roll out two small balls to attach with glue on the tops of the antennae, where a bit of spaghetti is sticking out.

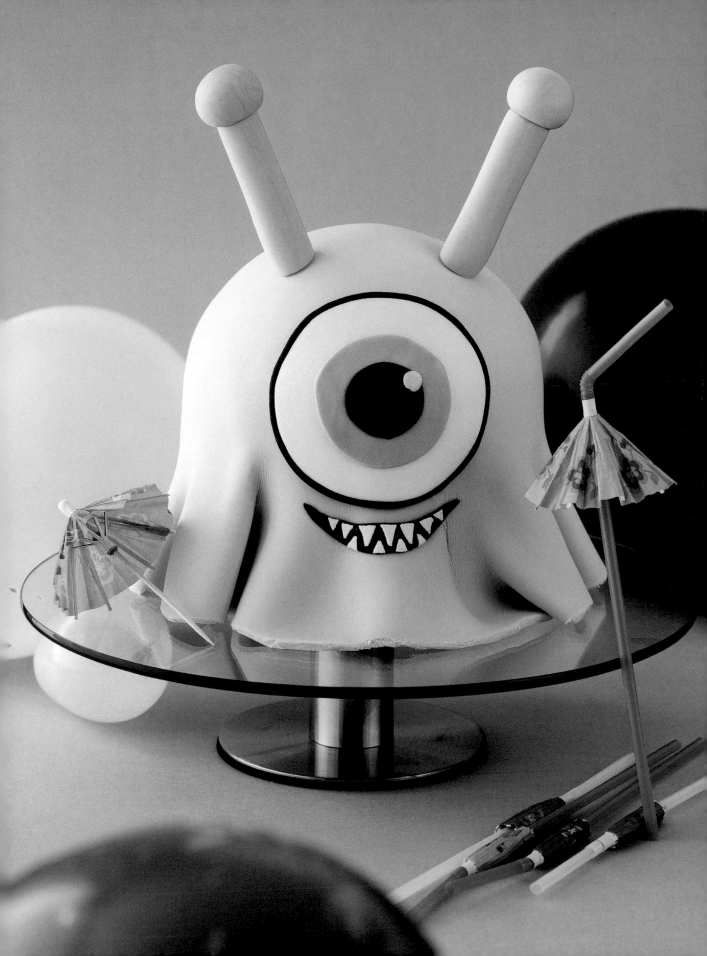

BASEBALL CAP CAKE

A baseball cap cake can be an option for kids, or
perhaps for dad. Maybe junior has a favorite cap you
can copy? This is a suggestion for how to make a cap,
but you can easily decorate it with the birthday boy
or girl's favorite logo, be it a hip-hop cap, a gangster
cap, a New Era cap, or something else.

Here's what you do:

- ♥ If you want to fill the cake with a crème, use only a thin layer, so the cake doesn't lose its shape.
- ♥ Cover the cake with a thin layer of crème.
- ♥ Roll out the blue material and cover the cake. Place it on a dish. Cut out the brim of the cap and place it against the cake.
- ♥ Make lines on the cap, six lines that all meet at the top of the cap.
- ♥ Use a tool with teeth to make seams on either side of each line. Also make a seam along the edge of the brim.
- ♥ Roll out a ball of red material and press it slightly flat. Glue it in place on top of the cap where the lines meet.
- ♥ Roll out a bit of red material and make a C, for Chicago Cubs. Cut out a circle and a smaller circle from within the first, so you have a letter O. Cut away a bit on the right, so you're left with a C. Glue it to the front of the cap.

You need:

a cake base cooked in
half a sports ball mold

blue, and a bit of red,
decorating material

a cutting wheel

modeling tools: one with
teeth to make seams,
and one with a slightly
sharp edge to make lines

two circular cutters of
different sizes

edible glue

a brush

Ball-shaped Mold

COLORFUL SWEET CAKE

This pastel-colored cake in two tiers is something for all children. You can make this cake in the colors the birthday boy or girl likes best. Gum balls are attached around the edges of the cake for a colorful element.

You need:

a round cake, 8 inches (20 cm) in diameter, and another, 6 inches (15 cm) in diameter

wooden sticks and a cardboard disc

pink, purple, and white decorating material

a cutting wheel

gum balls in different colors

edible glue

a brush

birthday candles in different colors

Here's what you do:

♥ Fill the cakes and cover them with a thin layer of crème. They'll look nicest if the cakes are the same height. The small cake goes on a cardboard disc of the exact same diameter as the cake itself. It shouldn't be visible, but should rather function as a support when the cakes are stacked.

♥ Roll out the purple material and cover the large cake base. Place the cake on a dish. Roll out white material, a bit larger than the diameter of the cake. Try placing the baking pan on top of the white material, so you have a guide to work with. Take a cutting wheel and cut in waves around the pan. Attach the white material to the purple cover, so that the waves come over the edge of the cake.

♥ Roll out the pink material and cover the small cake. Roll out white material and repeat the same process as for the large cake.

♥ Cut three wooden or plastic sticks to push into the lower cake. Place the small cake on top of the large cake. Make sure you place the small cake right in the middle of the large one; use a ruler to measure.

♥ Cover the edge between the two cakes by gluing on the gum balls. You can also roll your own balls out of fondant or marzipan and attach these around the cake instead.

♥ Roll some balls of pink and purple material, the same number of balls as you have candles. Place them in a circle on top of the cake and fasten them with edible glue. Carefully press a candle into each one.

BARBIE CAKE

All girls who like Barbie will love this cake. The Barbie doll in the cake becomes an extra gift for the birthday child once the cake has been eaten.

a cake baked in a wonder-mold form, or two 6 inch (15 cm) cakes

a Barbie doll and plastic wrap

red and white decorating material

a cutting wheel

a small flower-shaped cutter

pink sugar pearls

Wondermold form

Barbie covered in plastic wrap

Here's what you do:

♥ Use the wonder-mold cake, or stack two 6 inch (15 cm) cakes on top of each other; cut them to make a dress shape.

♥ Take off Barbie's clothes and cover the legs with plastic wrap. You can wrap the clothes and give them to the birthday child as a gift. You can also take the legs off entirely and use just the torso, if you feel it'd be easier. (You can put the legs back on later.)

♥ Cut a hole in the middle of the cake; use a spoon to scoop out a little bit of the inside. Put the Barbie doll in the hole and make sure she fits into the cake.

♥ Take the doll out. Fill the cake and cover it with a thin layer of crème. Make sure the hole isn't covered by the filling.

♥ Roll eight cylinders of fondant in two different thicknesses, thinner on the ends than in the middle. Fasten these around the cake before putting on the cover. Place the four thickest ones with the same distance between them, and attach the thinner ones in the space between the thicker ones. They should be attached so that they go vertically down the cake. The point of attaching these is to make it easier to add waves to the dress. The dress looks more natural with a bit of life to it.

♥ Place a covering over the cake, and let it fall between the cylinders you attached. Use clean hands to shape the dress to fit the cake. Use a cutting wheel to cut away any excess material, but remember that the dress should go a bit beyond the edge of the cake, such that you don't cut all the way up to it.

♥ Roll out more pink material for the upper part of the dress. Here, I've made a top with a strap decorated with flowers and sugar pearls. The material can be fastened to the dress without issue, so you don't need any glue. Use a hobby knife to cut it out right after covering the top of Barbie with the material. Make sure the seam is even on the back.

♥ Place the doll in the cake where you made the hole.

♥ Cut out two semicircles from the material, placing them on either side of the dress for a bit of flair. Cut out a white strip to glue around the waist of the doll, which covers the separation between the dress and the doll nicely. Make a bow with the help of a bow-shaped form, or make a simple one yourself to glue on the back.

♥ Decorate Barbie with some extras, like a handbag or hairpins, if you have them. You can also make a fine, festive hairstyle on the doll.

HANDBAG CAKE

This cake is shaped like a handbag. If the birthday child or other celebrant has a favorite brand, you can cut out the logo and attach it to the bag for a more personalized cake.

You need:

a cake baked in a small, long pan

white and black material

modeling paste

spaghetti

a flower-shaped cutter

black sugar pearls

a sugar gun

a cutting wheel

edible glue

a brush

Here's what you do:

♥ Cut a small long-pan cake into three pieces of equal size. Place them on top of each other with filling in between. Cut the cake into a trapezoidal shape, where the top is narrower than the bottom. Cut the edges and corners to be a bit round, so that the borders of the cake aren't so sharp. Cover the cake with a thin layer of crème.

♥ Roll out a cylinder of modeling paste for the handle of the bag. Measure the width of the cake and bend the handle with the same width between its ends. Push two spaghetti pieces in each end of the handle and leave it to dry.

♥ Roll out the white material and cover the cake.

♥ Cut out a cover for the bag, consisting of a square and a semicircle. It should be as wide as the top of the cake. Place it over the top of the cake.

♥ Use a sugar gun to press out a border to put around the cover, so that it's visually distinguishable from the rest of the bag.

♥ Cover the lower corners with triangles and the edge with a black border.

♥ Make a flower out of white and black material to decorate the bag. Decorate the flower with sugar pearls. Glue it in the middle and slightly below the horizontal center of the cover of the bag.

♥ Attach the handle to the bag, which should have stiffened a bit by now. If it's not stiff enough, let it sit and dry a while longer. Put a bit of edible glue on the ends of the handle, and then set it in place. The spaghetti pieces will help to hold it on, so it doesn't slip.

FLOWER POT CAKE

How about some edible flowers as a birthday gift? This cake takes out two birds with one stone—it's a cake and flowers at the same time.

You need:

two cake bases, 6 inches (15 cm) in diameter

a sharp knife

white, green, and purple decorating material

a cutting wheel

a leaf-shaped cutter

a flower-shaped cutter

large pearl-white sugar pearls, ¼ inch (7 mm)

edible glue

a brush

Here's what you do:

♥ Fill the cakes and place them on top of each other.

♥ Draw a circle on a piece of paper, 4 inches (10 cm) in diameter. Cut it out and place it on top of the cake, in the center. Cut from this circle out to the edge and down, cutting so that the flower pot is narrower at the bottom and wider at the top. But remember that right now, you have the bottom of the flower pot turned up.

♥ When you're happy with the shape, spread a thin layer of crème over the cake.

♥ Roll out some white material and cover the cake. Cut out a strip to glue along the bottom of the cake, as it currently stands. Try pushing a flower-shaped cutter into this strip, so you get a pattern around the whole border.

♥ Bring out the cake dish you want to use and place it upside-down on the cake; then, turn the cake upside down, so that the thinnest part of the cake is now on the bottom.

♥ Roll out green material and cut out shapes with a leaf-shaped cutter. Attach these to the top of the cake and let them fall outside the edge of the flower pot.

♥ Roll out purple material and cut out flowers. Glue a sugar pearl in the center of each.

♥ Place the flowers on top of the leaves.

TIP

You can make the flowers in whatever color you like; use several colors if you want to. If you don't have a flower-shaped cutter, you can use a piping tip to press out circles, or you can roll small balls to press and arrange into flowers.

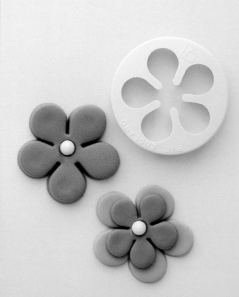

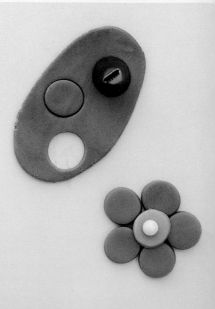

Square-shaped Form

You need:

a square cake, 8 x 8 inches (20 x 20 cm)

red and white decorating material

modeling paste

a sugar gun

a heart-shaped cutter

edible glue

a brush

PRESENT CAKE

This cake looks like a wrapped gift and fits in well at a birthday. Perhaps you'll bring along an edible gift next time you go to a party?

Here's what you do:

♥ Start by making the loops. You should make them at least a day in advance.

♥ Roll out the modeling paste and cut out strips, about 4¾ x 1 inch (12 x 3 cm).

♥ Put glue on the ends of these and fold them together. Place them on their sides and make an elliptical opening in the loops. Make twelve, in case some end up breaking. It's always wise to make a few extra.

♥ When they've dried and stiffened up, cut off the ends, to make them sharp. But cut carefully, so that the bows aren't destroyed. The reason for this is that they're easier to put together when the ends are sharp.

♥ Use a sugar gun to make cylinders of red material, which you glue on to the edges of the loops, on both sides. When you're done, set them aside.

♥ Fill the cake and cover it with a thin layer of crème.

♥ Roll out the red material and cover the cake. Roll out two strips of white material in the same width as the loops. Place these over the cake in a cross, as packaging ribbons.

♥ Cut out small red hearts, gluing these onto the ribbons on the cake.

♥ Now, start on the bow. It should sit on top of the cake, where the ribbons cross each other. Use edible glue to attach the bands to the cake. Place four loops on the base, and four more on top of the others, such that they fall in between the first loops. Finally, place one loop on top. You might need to cut away a bit of the end of each loop in order for there to be room for it without sticking too high up.

1.

2.

3.

4.

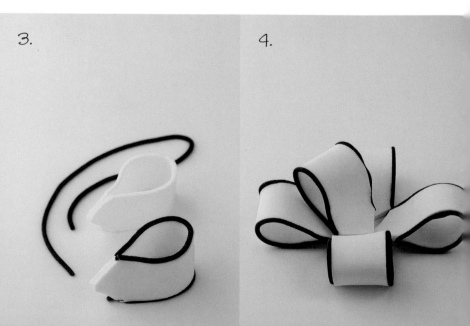

COFFEE CUP CAKE

This cake is shaped like a coffee cup. Perhaps the celebrant has their own favorite cup you can copy the design from? This is two cakes stacked on top of each other.

You need:

two cake bases, 6 inches (15 cm) in diameter

white material for the cup

purple, orange, yellow, pink, and green material for the circles

red material for the letters

letter-shaped cutters

modeling paste for the handle

spaghetti

a cutting wheel

a sheet of melted dark chocolate

edible glue

a brush

Here's what you do:

♥ Stack two cakes, 6 inches (15 cm) in diameter, atop each other.
♥ Roll out a cylinder of modeling paste and make a C shape for the handle. Stick two pieces of spaghetti in each end. Set it aside to dry.
♥ Fill and cover the cake with a thin layer of crème.
♥ Cut out a rectangle in the white material, about half an inch (1 cm) taller than the cake and as long as the circumference of the cake. Cover the sides of the cake with this rectangle. Make sure the ends are cut so that they meet, rather than overlapping. Use a cake smoother to even out the surface.
♥ Pour the melted chocolate over the top of the cake. There should be a small edge around the top of the cake so the chocolate doesn't overflow. Distribute the chocolate evenly on top, but make sure not to cross the edge.
♥ Roll out the red material and cut out "CONGRATULATIONS" using the letter-shaped cutters. Glue these letters onto the cup.
♥ Roll out the purple, pink, yellow, orange, and green material and cut out lots of circles of the same size. Glue these to the cup around the text.
♥ Put a bit of glue on the ends of the handle and attach it to the side of the cup. The spaghetti will help hold it in place.

STORES AND ONLINE STORES

There are several online and brick-and-mortar stores in Norway that sell cake equipment. If you buy your equipment from another country, you can count on tolls and fees in addition to the shipping and actual price of the equipment, so it's not always the best option. I recommend these stores:

Cacas

www.cacas.no
Kongens gate 14, Oslo
They have a large selection of everything you need for cake baking and decorating. They carry a large assortment of Wilton products.

Jernia

www.jernia.no
Jernia often has a stand in stores with coloring paste and other small items for decorating. They also sell lots of baking equipment.

Kakeboksen

www.kakeboksen.no.
They have a good selection, good service, and sell things a good deal more affordably than other cake stores.

Søte saker

www.sotesaker.no
Online store with a large selection of cake equipment.

Traktøren

www.traktoren.no
Traktøren is a retailer that sells lots of baking equipment.

Thanks

The publisher would like to thank the following stores for loaning out their equipment: Ting, Tilbords, Åhlens, Illums Bolighus, Rafens, Christiana Glasmagasin, Jernia, Standard, and Cacas.

Author's thanks:
Thank you to my son, Sondre, who is both my regular taste-tester, and the actual reason I began baking decorative birthday cakes and trying out new cake ideas.